MINNESOTA
GEOGRAPHIC SERIES
NO. 3

CONNIE WANNER

MINNESOTA BACKROADS

BY JOHN G. SHEPARD

AMERICAN GEOGRAPHIC PUBLISHING

WILLIAM A. CORDINGLEY, CHAIRMAN
RICK GRAETZ, PUBLISHER & CEO
MARK O. THOMPSON, DIRECTOR OF PUBLICATIONS
BARBARA FIFER, PRODUCTION MANAGER

D0878743

FOR SUZANNE

John G. Shepard is a full-time free-lance travel and outdoor writer and photographer whose work has appeared in dozens of national and regional magazines and in the travel sections of prominent daily newspapers across the country. He and his wife, daughter and son live in St. Paul.

Library of Congress Cataloging-in-Publication Data

Shepard, John G.
  Minnesota backroads / by John G. Shepard.
      p.   cm. -- (Minnesota geographic series : no. 3)
  Includes bibliographical references (p.   ).
  ISBN 0-938314-77-7 : $15.95
  1. Minnesota--Description and travel--1981- --Tours. I. Title. II. Title: Minnesota back roads. III. Series
F604.3.S52   1990
917.7604'53--dc20   89-18626
                              CIP

American Geographic Publishing is a corporation for publishing illustrated geographic information and guides. It is not associated with American Geographical Society. It has no commercial or legal relationship to and should not be confused with any other company, society or group using the words geographic or geographical in its name or its publications.

ISBN 0-938314-77-7

GLENN VAN NIMWEGEN

INTRODUCTION

CHRIS POLYDOROFF

Minnesota and I celebrated our 35th wedding anniversary in 1989, and it's clear to me that the marriage is much healthier now, in its middle age, than it ever has been. Understand, ours has always been a very good relationship. Yet, before I undertook the task of researching this book, I would say that I was pretty much sleep-walking through life with my bride.

She was *so* familiar to me. I'd been in her presence almost continually since the moment of my birth. Most of my free time had been spent with her and we'd been close working partners in several jobs that I'd held. I knew her to be a terrific playmate, a productive worker and a hospitable host who historically has been generous with her extensive resources almost to a fault. I often was moved by her great beauty and I always enjoyed the wide range of her seasonal moods, though, frankly, I admit that Minnesota's occasional January rains disappoint the skier in me. Still, I can say without reservation that I've always been proud to be a Minnesotan.

But now that I've taken the time to *really* get to know her—to travel many of her back roads that wind through a surprisingly complex geography and a fascinating history—I can see I'd only just begun to plumb the depths of who she really is and appreciate all that she has to offer. My admiration for my home state has deepened immeasurably as a result, and I can see that in our remaining years together there is still much more territory to be explored and many more stories to be discovered.

It is my intention that by reading this book you might be instilled with some of this heightened appreciation of the North Star State and delight with me in uncovering some of her more intriguing qualities. Also, whether you're a life-long Minnesota resident like me, or a newcomer, I hope that these pages will kindle a desire to discover for yourself, traveling at your own pace and following your own interests, all that Minnesota is eager to share with those willing to take the road less traveled.

As you venture off the beaten path, you will learn first-hand about the profound impact that our civilization has had upon Minnesota's ever-giving lands and waters. It will be evident that our activities and industries often have not been motivated by the spirit of profound respect and stewardship that so rich a gift of nature deserves. I encourage you to undertake your visits as if you were an honored guest in the grand household of a highly esteemed relative. If you're moved by what you find, you can return the favor by advocating for conservation those precious resources that remain. Minnesota and future Minnesotans will appreciate your concern, and you can justly take pride in being a member of so illustrious a family.

Each of the book's 12 chapters revolves around a particularly interesting aspect of Minnesota's wide-ranging geography and history. While far from exhausting all that there is to explore in these regions, each chapter brings to light those features of the environment, its people and its past that are especially intriguing to me—hence this is a very personal book. It is not intended as a travel guide, though many specific sites of interest are located and described. (To assist you in finding information to guide you in your travels, reference information is provided at the back of the book.) Rather, *Minnesota Backroads* is an unabashed tribute—an informed celebration—in words and pictures of the state that is Minnesota.

J.G.S.
April 1989
St. Paul, Minnesota

Above: *The grand valley of the Mississippi River is steeped in history, rich in wildlife, and offers plentiful recreational opportunities.*
Facing page: *Formidable 100-foot quartzite cliffs rising over the top of a ragged line of oaks greeted westward-bound settlers at the Blue Mounds (now Blue Mounds State Park).*

Title page: *The moods of Lake Superior—from the infinite calm of August's doldrums to the furious northeasters in late autumn—befit an ocean more than a land-locked freshwater sea.*

Front cover: R. HAMILTON SMITH PHOTO

Back cover, top left: *Split Rock Lighthouse, Lake Superior.*
MIKE MAGNUSON
Top right: RICHARD LONGSETH
Bottom: R. HAMILTON SMITH

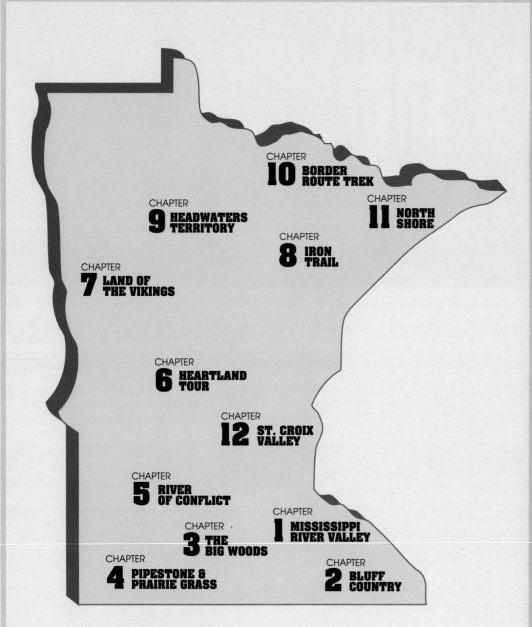

CHAPTER
10 BORDER ROUTE TREK

CHAPTER
11 NORTH SHORE

CHAPTER
9 HEADWATERS TERRITORY

CHAPTER
8 IRON TRAIL

CHAPTER
7 LAND OF THE VIKINGS

CHAPTER
6 HEARTLAND TOUR

CHAPTER
12 ST. CROIX VALLEY

CHAPTER
5 RIVER OF CONFLICT

CHAPTER
1 MISSISSIPPI RIVER VALLEY

CHAPTER
3 THE BIG WOODS

CHAPTER
4 PIPESTONE & PRAIRIE GRASS

CHAPTER
2 BLUFF COUNTRY

MIKE MAGNUSON

CONTENTS

Clockwise from top left:

Steam engines of every size and description are on display and in action at the Western Minnesota Steam Threshers Reunion in Rollag. Touted as the largest such gathering in the world, the reunion draws as many as to 80,000 visitors each Labor Day weekend.

Northern Minnesota's extensive pine forests supported a massive logging industry around the turn of the century. The harvesting of birch and aspen continues where towering white and red pine once stood.

Built between 1819 and 1825 as Minnesota's first permanent structure, historic Fort Snelling still dominates the confluence of the Mississippi and Minnesota rivers. Daily, from May through October, a contingent of soldiers re-enact with humor and robust spirit the highly regimented and often tedious life led by the fort's early inhabitants.

Steelhead, salmon and smelt attract anglers to the many rivers and streams that tumble downhill through the Sawtooth Mountains along Minnesota's Lake Superior North Shore.

August Schell built this New Ulm mansion in 1885 as a monument to his successful family brewery. Tours of the historic and still-prosperous Schell Brewery are offered in the summer months.

DANIEL J. COX   MIKE MAGNUSON

**La Crescent
Hastings
Red Wing
Frontenac State Park
Lake Pepin
Winona**

Above: *Historic riverboats still ply the Mississippi. Paddle wheelers like the* Delta Queen *recreate a lavish lifestyle reminiscent of the life and times of river pilot/author Mark Twain.*

Facing page: *The view from the top of Barn Bluff, a protrusion of ancient sandstone carved by a glacial Mississippi River near what is now downtown Red Wing, has changed little since it was visited by Henry David Thoreau in 1861.*

MISSISSIPPI RIVER VALLEY

For a family of early settlers traveling upstream on the Mississippi River aboard a crowded steamboat, entering southeastern Minnesota's Hiawatha Valley must have been a thrill. From their embarkation at St. Louis, through Illinois and into Iowa, the banks of America's mightiest river were low, the surrounding countryside was flat and the landscape was dominated by the wide expanse of swirling, silty currents moving quickly sternward. Then the course of the river narrowed and on either bank gradually emerged, from the flatlands, parallel ramparts of steep wooded bluffs rising hundreds of feet in the sky. Cliffs stood out above stately oaks, revealing bands of crumbling sandstone and dolomite formed millions of years ago when the region was submerged by a warm and shallow sea.

These imposing bluffs were dissected by deep ravines. In their shadows were clear-flowing rivers that served as highways into the dense hardwood forests and rolling prairies to the west. Except for the raw beginnings of river towns like Winona, Wabasha and Red Wing—all of whose names derive from regional Dakota and Ojibway Indian lore—the river valley was pristine and untamed. The woods were teeming with deer and wild turkey and the crystalline waters of the Zumbro, Root, Whitewater and Cannon rivers were ripe with trout.

During the settlement boom of the mid- to late-1800s, most riverboat traffic on the Mississippi was destined for the head of navigation at St. Paul—a burgeoning river town whose early history, as Mark Twain has noted, betrayed the sanctity that its name suggests. For the driving force of civilization at the site of Minnesota's capital-to-be was not the steamboat, the railroad, the newspaper or the missionary. No, it was a rogue named Pierre "Pig's Eye" Parrant and his whisky.

Twain's dictum is that "Westward the Jug of Empire takes its way" and, sure enough, in 1837 Parrant established a saloon on the banks of the Mississippi, around which a motley settlement slowly grew. A few years later a missionary was attracted to the site—a Roman Catholic named Father Lucian Galtier—who, from the pulpit of his log chapel, succeeded in bestowing upon the place the first strains of civilization along with a respectable alternative to the name then in use: "Pig's Eye."

The four-hour drive from St. Paul downstream to La Crescent is enough to convince today's travelers that, fortunately for us, the features that drew pioneers to what was then the very edge of civilization have retained many of their special qualities. The oak-lined bluffs are as dramatic and inspiring as they were 100 years ago. The rivers that wend their way to mingle with the Father of Waters are still quite clean and rich with trout. The Mississippi itself—though polluted, channelized and harnessed by a series of locks and dams—still flows magnificently. It is a river that is as profoundly deep in historic significance as it is epic in its physical proportions.

The Mississippi offers great recreational opportunities, too, for adventuresome river rats, hunters and anglers, and for those whose notions of a holiday would be well served aboard a luxurious paddle wheeler in the Twain tradition. Moreover, the towns passed en route have retained much of their historic appeal through ongoing preservation efforts by citizens who recognize the great value in upholding the region's rich heritage.

Hastings—found near the junction of the Mississippi, St. Croix, and Vermillion rivers—is the first of these lovely river towns to be encountered when driving The Great River Road (Route 61) south along the Mississippi from the Twin Cities.

LEFT: MARK E. GIBSON; BELOW: CLEO FREELANCE PHOTO

The town was first known as Oliver's Grove after a military officer, Lt. William Oliver, whose supply barge became stranded for the winter at this site in 1819. A young soldier in Oliver's company at the time, 14-year-old Joseph R. Brown, returned a dozen years later to establish a trading post that eventually grew into a village.

By the mid-19th century, the growing settlement was re-named Hastings after Minnesota's first governor, Henry Hastings Sibley, and began to prosper from the churning water-powered grain mills, such as the one that is now a stone ruin in Vermilion Falls Park. The business generated by the area's booming agriculture gave this little city of 13,000 a reputation as one of the largest wheat markets in the Northwest.

Today, the ornate store fronts on Second Avenue,

located beneath the south end of the Route 61 bridge, and the town's many well preserved Victorian homes beautifully preserve some flavor of how Hastings looked when the town's economic life revolved around its levee. Among the many houses worth exploring here, perhaps the most noteworthy is the Minnesota Historical Society-owned LeDuc-Simmons mansion—one of America's best remaining examples of a Hudson River Gothic Revival style residence.

Route 61 leads south out of Hastings on a flat agricultural plateau that shortly drops down a ravine to follow the wooded shoreline of the Mississippi. But before the Big Muddy is in sight, the highway crosses the Cannon River—a lovely, clear canoeing stream with an accompanying 19-mile bicycle/skiing path along an old railroad grade. Using this path, self-powered adventurers can cover the distance from Cannon Falls to Red Wing.

The Cannon cuts a meandering course through a deep, tree-lined valley with high bluffs. Deadfalls and collected branches swept downstream during spring runoff, and occasional sections of fast water—there are no rapids—create some challenging obstacles for beginning canoeists. Gusty spring winds, channeled between the river valley's steep walls, also occasionally create some unexpected effects for the unprepared paddler. Birders, anglers and picnickers will also find the Cannon River valley to be a great site for an afternoon's get-away. Canoe and inner-tube rentals are available at the little riverside town of Welch, where a couple of antique shops also proffer their wares.

The city of Red Wing, once known nationally for the production of excellent stoneware under the Red Wing label, now offers visitors some wonderful opportunities to escape into the past. In the mid- to late-19th century, this city of 15,000 outdid Hastings in its ability to attract business related to the area's burgeoning wheat market. And to accommodate the high rollers who came via riverboat to Red Wing on business, in 1875 a top-quality hotel was built, known then and now as the St. James.

A thorough restoration in 1979 succeeded in bringing the St. James back to life in all its former splendor, adding the modern conveniences that today's travelers expect. Excellent continental meals are served by teams of attentive waiters in the St. James' Victorian Room (one of three restaurants in the hotel). For those seeking more intimate accommodations, there also are several bed and breakfasts establishments in town that provide fine settings for a special getaway.

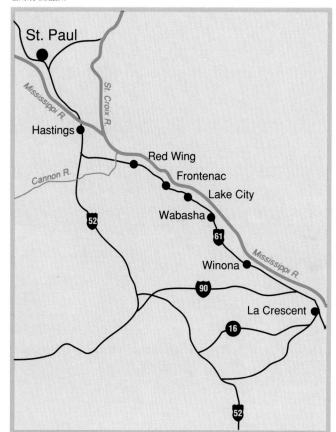

LINDA COLLINS

No matter where you stay, a night on the town in Red Wing would do well to include a cinematic, theatrical, dramatic or musical performance at the fabulous T.B. Sheldon Theater. The Beaux Arts-style Sheldon is another architectural gem, this one dating from the turn of the century, that recently has been gloriously resurrected. Stained glass windows, ornate decorative plaster and grand curved staircases have given the Sheldon a reputation as a "jewel box" theater. Where vaudeville used to fill the stage, today you can expect nationally known classical and popular concerts, film festivals and acclaimed drama.

Red Wing's picturesque location, at the base of the bluffs beside the twisting channels of the Mississippi, can be most fully appreciated by a hike to the top of Barn Bluff—a mountain carved by a much-enlarged glacial Mississippi millennia

MARK E. GIBSON

Right: Red Wing, another quiet Mississippi River town, nourishes a historic reputation as a major wheat market and a source of distinctive stoneware that once dominated the industry.

Facing page, top: Red Wing's St. James Hotel was built in 1875 to accommodate businessmen traveling up and down the river. Today three excellent restaurants, and a faithful renovation featuring antiques and antique reproductions, preserve for the St. James a well deserved reputation as one of the state's finest historic hotels.

Bottom: The fine woodwork and Victorian furnishings of the St. James Hotel library lure guests for a quiet game of chess or a chance to read beside the open fire.

ago. Starting at the east end of Fifth Street just south of downtown, trails leading to the top and along the sides of Barn Bluff offer great vistas of the town nestled between the bluffs and the braided river.

Not far downstream of Red Wing, commanding a panoramic view of 22-mile-long Lake Pepin—a riverine "lake" formed by the natural damming of the Mississippi by the effluent-heavy delta of its tributary Chippewa River—is a wonderful state park. It shares the name of a nearby settlement, Frontenac, in honor of the man who served as governor of New France from 1671 to 1698. In its heyday in

the late 19th century, the little community of Frontenac was an exclusive retreat where high-society folk from New Orleans, St. Louis and St. Paul came to enjoy the area's pastoral charm, great vistas and fine hunting. Many of the original stately homes and the old Lake Side Inn (now Chateau Frontenac—a condo complex) can be seen today.

Frontenac State Park provides more than 13 miles of hiking, snowmobiling, and skiing trails winding through a rugged landscape that has been occupied by various cultural groups for well over 2,000 years. Perched high up near the edge of the bluff is a giant boulder—In-Yan-Teopa Rock—

10

CLEO FREELANCE PHOTO

TIM GRAY

The wonderful Frontenac State Park honors the memory of the governor of New France who served from 1671 to 1698.

that was a sacred site to local Dakota and Fox Indians. A picnic area with panoramic views of the valley is located nearby.

With Lake Pepin's waves lapping invitingly at its doorstep, Lake City is a likely place for people to become innovative with water sports. It was here in 1922 that a young man named Ralph Samuelson was inspired to strap eight-foot pine boards on his feet and allow himself to be towed behind a speeding motorboat for the first time in history. Water skiing still prospers on Lake Pepin, as do sailing, fishing, houseboating and motorized cruising. Also, the precipitous bluffs behind this lakeshore community provide one of the state's best sites for hang gliding. Modern-day Icaruses frequently can be seen soaring high overhead, suspended only by their wings of cloth.

Winona, located still farther downstream on the Mississippi floodplain, is a larger town that offers rich architecture

Left The T.B. Sheldon Theatre has been lovingly restored to its former splendor as a concert and performance hall that entertained Red Wing residents for much of this century.

Below: The valley of the Cannon River, one of several lovely streams that flow through hardwood bluff country into the Mississippi, draws canoeists, inner tubers and cyclists during the warmer months. The 19-mile bike path, which follows an old railroad grade, is groomed as a cross-country ski trail in winter.

Facing page: Lake Pepin, a natural reservoir of the Mississippi River, was formed by debris washing into the Mississippi from Wisconsin's Chippewa River, which created a constrictive narrows. Wooded bluffs overlooking the lake attract hang gliders, while Pepin's open waters are a playground for sailors.

The Winona area annually is visited by more than 280 varieties of birds.

Right: *In-Yan-Teopa rock, high atop the riverside bluffs of Frontenac State Park, long has been considered a sacred site by the Dakota and Fox Indians who hunted the area when the first Europeans arrived.*

Facing page: *Oaks, birches and other hardwoods adorn a spectacular picnic area high above the Mississippi River in Frontenac State Park. Miles of hiking, skiing and snowmobiling trails wind through a river bluff environment that is rich in history and natural beauty. Archaeological excavations in the park date the earliest inhabitants to about the time of Christ's birth.*

and a well preserved sense of history. Its name derives from the legend of a Dakota maiden named We-no-nah who was forced by her parents to enter into an arranged marriage although she loved another. In her grief We-no-nah leapt to her death from Maiden's Rock, a cliff on what is now the Wisconsin shoreline of Lake Pepin. (Unless one takes Mark Twain's version to be the truth: that is, the young maiden threw herself upon her parents and dashed *them* to pieces. "She was a good deal jarred up and jolted," he writes, "but she got herself together and disappeared before the coroner reached the fatal spot.")

The Mississippi River forms one of North America's greatest waterfowl flyways, and the Winona area annually is

visited by more than 280 varieties of birds. The Trempealeau Refuge, about six miles downstream from Winona's park-like levee, is a favorite destination among birders, particularly during the spring and fall migrations. A road winds for about six miles through forest and marsh lands, traversing habitat that supports lark sparrows, grouse, bluebirds, double-crested cormorants, bitterns, geese, ducks and osprey as well as the grand birds of prey: hawks and bald eagles. The best times to visit the refuge are in the early morning and late afternoon.

Pickwick Mill
Schech's Mill
Root River
Chatfield
Lanesboro
Rushford Village
Mystery Cave

Above: O.L. Kipp State Park, a popular natural area in the Mississippi River valley, draws hikers, skiers and birds to its rugged hills and valleys.
Facing page: Cumbersome towboats and barges ply the Mississippi today just as they have for over 100 years. Motorists can find scenic outlooks along Route 61 and on back roads that wind up steep ravines to the top of the bluffs.

BLUFF COUNTRY

Minnesota's bluff country is a geological anomaly. Everywhere else you go in the state you are witness to a landscape that was profoundly affected by the glaciers of the last ice age. It's estimated that in some places the glacial ice flowing southward into Minnesota from the arctic regions of North America 10,000 to 20,000 years ago was as much as a mile thick. That's right, a *mile* thick. There are places where the bedrock has been estimated to have been compacted by as much as 300 meters from the sheer pressure of all that ice. If you're ever given to wonder why there are no mountains worthy of the name in Minnesota, this information should do nicely for an answer.

But while thousands of years of glacial crunching, gouging and scraping were occurring everywhere else in Minnesota, the southeastern corner of the state came through the ordeal unscathed. The creeping rivers of ice routed themselves around the area that scientists now call the "driftless zone"—an oasis of steep hills and intimate valleys south and east of Rochester, to this day alive with dense hardwood forests, rare (for Minnesota) wildlife and pristine rivers. It is a beautiful region that resembles sections of the mountainous states in the eastern part of the country more than it does the rest of Minnesota.

There is in most southern Minnesotans—at least among those living in the Twin Cities—an instinctual tendency to gravitate northward whenever short opportunities present themselves to escape the hubbub of daily life. Everyone heads "up north" to "the lake" where "the cabin" sits in waiting. Relatively few make the short drive south into the bluff country where a whole new realm of experience awaits.

My discovery of the bluff country began when I ventured south from Winona and up a steep draw past one of the oldest water-powered mills in the state. The seven-story limestone Pickwick Mill, built in 1854, is remarkable for its endurance—it has survived one major flood and a tornado that took off its roof—and for its unusual method of construction. The structural support provided by heavy wooden beams and columns is accomplished without the use of a single nail. Rather, the weight of the stone walls and the careful placement of these wooden parts are credited for the mill's stalwartness.

A second mill in the heart of the bluff country is even more intriguing. Schech's water-powered grist mill, near Sheldon on the outskirts of Beaver Creek Valley State Park, is the oldest water mill in the state that still functions to support the day-to-day operations of a working farm. Ivan Krugmire, the owner of the farm on which this 1876-vintage creation thrives, offers tours from spring through summer—and a real farmer's tour it is. Ivan chats on about the intricacies of the turbine; the huge leather belts that spin axles, gears and assorted other whirring devices; and the various types of grist his outfit is capable of turning out. Then he opens the floodgates and sets the whole building a-shudder as the big millstones do their work.

The waters that flow through the bluff country are not now, nor have they ever been, suitable only for powering machines. That special breed of angler whose instincts are especially excited by the wily trout has found this part of the state to be prime territory to pursue his or her sport. Bluff country is laced with dozens of exceptionally clear, secluded

LINDA COLLINS

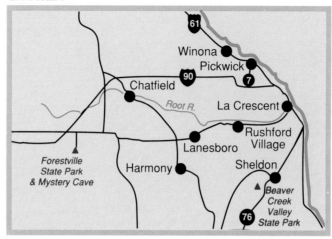

Explore the Root River by canoe, or on foot, or by bicycling along a 35-mile converted railroad grade.

streams that offer both natural and stocked specimens of brookies, browns and rainbows. One of Minnesota's largest trout hatcheries is located at Lanesboro, providing an interesting tour for those enamored of or wishing to learn more about this special breed of fish.

Of all the winding streams in the region, the Root River is perhaps the best known and most frequently visited. From Chatfield to the river's confluence with the Mississippi south of La Crescent, a distance of 90 miles, the Root has been officially designated by the Department of Natural Resources as one of the state's prime canoe routes. Each spring and summer its clear, cool waters host weekend expeditioners, overnight adventurers and those out for a more leisurely afternoon paddle. The most remote section of the river runs from just downstream of Chatfield to Lanesboro—a perfect weekend trip where, for more than 30 miles, no roads parallel the river and only a couple of bridges ford it.

While exploring the Root—by canoe, on foot, or bicycling along a 35-mile converted railroad grade called the Root River State Trail—keep an eye open to the high bluffs on either side to catch glimpses of osprey and eagles in flight. A hike into the hills occasionally results in glimpses of the shy eastern timber rattlesnake—the only place in Minnesota where you're likely to find this critter outside a zoo.

Springtime finds fungus hunters scouring the damp forest floor in search of the official state mushroom—the edible morel—while in autumn the bluffs are a popular

JIM GALEWSKI

JIM GALEWSKI

Far left: *When constructed in 1854, Pickwick Mill was one of Minnesota's first industrial sites. This sturdy limestone building, held together without a single nail, survived a major flood and a tornado to serve the needs of Union soldiers in the Civil War.*
Left: *The Root River and many of its clear, cool tributaries offer some of the best trout fishing to be found anywhere.*
Below: *Minnesota's oldest unadulterated, fully functional water-powered gristmill can be found near Beaver Creek Valley State Park near Caledonia. Farmer Ivan Krugmire, owner and operator of Schech's Mill (circa 1876), offers tours during the summer.*

CONNIE WANNER

Hour-long tours of Mystery Cave provide a unique glimpse of the subterranean realm.

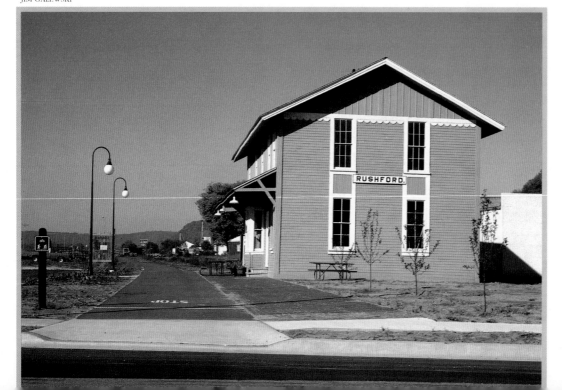

destination for hunters of wild turkey. During the winter the Root River State Trail is maintained for cross-country skiers. And not long after the snow melts the forest floor is sprinkled with delicate and colorful wildflowers.

Also awaiting discovery are a number of quaint historic towns nestled in the region's intimate valleys. Among the three most intriguing towns hidden along the banks of the Root River—Chatfield, Lanesboro and Rushford Village—Lanesboro is perhaps the most distinctive. Tightly crowded by precipitous tree-topped cliffs at a bend in the river and graced with enough historic commercial buildings and dwellings to be listed in its entirety on the National Register of Historic Places, Lanesboro is steeped in character and charm and has a number of unusual cultural attractions.

The Scenic Valley Winery, occupying an old creamery, produces a variety of cooking and table wines made of domestically-grown fruits. Tours and tasting at the winery are possible without special reservations. There is a blacksmith's forge, a woodcarver's studio and a shop specializing in locally-produced Amish crafts too. Several bed-and-break-

fast establishments offer hospitable and intimate lodgings, and dinner is served with continental flare at the Victorian House, a gourmet French restaurant occupying a grand Victorian *maison.*

The setting that inspired Meredith Willson's beloved musical, *The Music Man,* was Mason City, Iowa. But it might just as well have been the Root River town of Chatfield, for it was here in 1969 that an attorney named Jim Perkins undertook a project every bit as remarkable as Harold Hill's attempts to bring music to River City.

Perkins was in love with brass bands and he happened to live in a town that hadn't had one since World War II. So, following his decision to bring back the Chatfield Brass Band, he began collecting music from band leaders throughout the region. His collection of music soon grew so large that he and a group of fellow enthusiasts decided to share the wealth by establishing the Chatfield Brass Band Free Music Lending Library—the world's first and only institution of its kind.

The library, located at 81 Library Lane, has accumulated well more than 35,000 scores for all kinds of music and is contacted by bands and orchestras all around the world in search of hard-to-find music. Since its resurrection, the Chatfield band has gained national prominence too—and has shared the limelight with the world-class U.S. Marine Corps Band.

Brass band music lovers find it worthwhile to visit the library, where signed pictures of some of the country's great band music composers adorn the walls along with a collection of antique instruments. If you're in Chatfield at 7:30 any Thursday evening you can stop in at the high school auditorium where the Chatfield Brass Band holds their practices. Bring your own horn if you have one and come blow with some of Minnesota's best.

As a rule, rivers aren't supposed to disappear into an abyss, never to be seen again. And for the most part, the South Branch of the Root River flows serenely enough through the rolling hills of western Fillmore County in obedience to this principle—except at one place. On the outside of a gentle bend against a steep limestone bluff, part of the Root suddenly disappears into a hole in the ground. It was here in 1937 that a local farmer discovered the entrance to one of Minnesota's most intriguing natural attractions—Mystery Cave.

Today you can follow the footsteps of the cave's first explorers through a maze of interconnected caverns. Tours are led by naturalists from nearby Forestville State Park, which has been managing Mystery Cave since it was purchased by the Department of Natural Resources in 1988. These hour-long excursions provide a unique glimpse of the natural history of a fascinating subterranean realm.

Mystery Cave's intricate web of passageways winds for 12 miles through two distinct formations of ancient limestone. The rock of the 450-million-year-old Dubuque layer is shaped in huge rectangular blocks, creating square tunnel-like passages with large rooms and an occasional domed ceiling. Imbedded fossils of long-extinct marine organisms reflect the limestone's origins at the bottom of a prehistoric ocean. Passages in the deeper 500-million-year-old Galena limestone formation are crevasse-like, with undulating walls that reach to considerable heights.

The well lighted trail leads past a placid, crystal-clear turquoise lake. Small "rafts" of calcite float serenely on the surface, while the bottom and sides are lined with a mineral deposit appropriately called cave popcorn. "Living" towers of flowstone—still-growing formations of calcite deposited by seeping water—loom like colorful frozen waterfalls.

There are collections of large stalactites (icicle-like deposits) and stalagmites (similar creations that rise from the floor of the cave). And occasionally these calcite formations solidify into hanging sheets or "draperies" that eerily resemble living tissue. Although the 12 miles of known caverns qualify Mystery Cave as Minnesota's biggest cave and the 36th largest in the country, the system of passages hasn't been fully explored yet.

Naturalist-guided Mystery Cave tours begin at Forestville State Park, 12 miles southeast of Spring Valley on County Road 12, and are conducted daily through the summer.

Nearby is Niagara Cave, south of the little hamlet of Harmony off Highway 139 on Niagara Cave Road. Tours are also available at Niagara, which features a 60-foot waterfall.

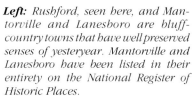

Left: *Rushford, seen here, and Mantorville and Lanesboro are bluff-country towns that have well preserved senses of yesteryear. Mantorville and Lanesboro have been listed in their entirety on the National Register of Historic Places.*
Below: *From the lookout at Garvin Heights Park, atop the limestone bluff 500 feet above Winona, many of the city's architectural attractions are visible against the backdrop of the Mississippi's twisting channels and the Wisconsin shoreline beyond.*

Facing page: *Rushford's historic railroad depot is an example of the rich architectural traditions preserved in the lovely Root River valley.*

Above: *This pre-Reformation stained glass window is in the Boe Chapel at St. Olaf College in Northfield.*

Facing page: *The dense hardwoods of Nerstrand Woods State Park are a remnant of the Big Woods that crossed central Minnesota in a great swath from northwest to southeast.*

THE BIG WOODS

Historic Fort Snelling occupies a commanding bluff-top position at the junction of the Minnesota and Mississippi rivers. Its low, thick limestone walls allow occupants to peer down into either river valley, where in bygone days cannon and muskets could be trained upon any interloper. However, as imposing as it is, the fort—which became Minnesota's first permanent structure upon completion in 1825—always has been a peaceful enough place. Never in its long history has a single shot been fired either in defense or attack.

Even so, every day each summer, a cadre of soldiers dressed in sweltering early 19th-century wool uniforms can be found dutifully marching in formation on the parade ground as they practice their mind-numbing drills, getting into various kinds of mischief and generally endeavoring to keep their fighting edge in case any hostile forces might threaten their remote frontier post. This Minnesota Historical Society-run historic site also has an excellent interpretive center with exhibits and films that relate to the fort and to the state's early history.

The fort and the river confluence below it, including Pike Island—considered by many Dakota to be the center of the world—form a geographic hub around which much of Minnesota's history has revolved. Minneapolis was founded a few miles upstream of this point on the Mississippi at the thundering Falls of St. Anthony. Approximately equal distance downstream, St. Paul established its prominence as the head of navigation on the Father of Waters.

In 1861, when steamboats regularly stopped at the wooded landing below the fort, a special visitor dropped in to have a look at Fort Snelling. Like many other cultured gentlemen traveling to the Twin Cities at the time, he made the obligatory visits to "St. Pauls," as he preferred to call the territorial capital, and the growing communities of St. Anthony and Minneapolis, which from opposite banks of the Mississippi had begun to tap the considerable waterpower of St. Anthony Falls for early lumber and milling industries.

Being of a literary bent, this fellow also visited a beautiful waterfall along a quiet creek between Minneapolis and Fort Snelling, called Minnehaha Falls (found today a couple blocks east of Hiawatha Avenue on Minnehaha Parkway). This landmark had attracted a certain fame with its prominent mention in the publication of Henry Wadsworth Longfellow's epic 1855 poem, *The Song of Hiawatha*. But, unlike Longfellow, who wrote his popular poem without ever having visited Minnehaha Falls or the "shining Big-Sea-water" of "Gitche Gumee" (Lake Superior), Henry David Thoreau elected to base his writings on the region upon his own astute observations and experiences.

Thoreau's journal of his Minnesota journey *(Thoreau's Minnesota Journey: Two Documents,* Thoreau Society, 1962) reflects the eye of a keen naturalist. Undertaking the trip a year before his death, he wasn't in the best of health during the voyage. Even so, his notes are filled with detailed observations of dozens of indigenous plants, trees and animals, and of the people he met on his travels.

From Fort Snelling, Thoreau took a five-day excursion by riverboat up the Minnesota River past the communities of Mankato and New Ulm to the Indian reservation at the Lower Sioux Agency. Here he spent some time with the Dakota, who had been restricted to reservation lands along the river for a decade. He took interest in the Indians' fire-starting techniques using flint and steel and he watched 30 Indian dancers moving in time to the rhythms produced by 12 drummers and a host of other onlookers, who struck arrows against their bows or played flutes.

Right and facing page: *Historic Fort Snelling is one of Minnesota's premier historic sites. The limestone structure has been reconstructed in painstaking detail, circa 1825, and Minnesota Historical Society staff in period dress bring to robust life the era when the northwestern frontier was a target of expansion.*

MARK E. GIBSON

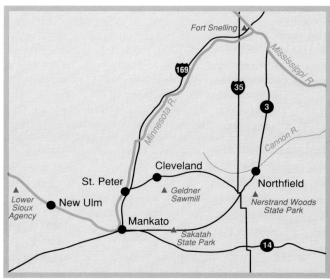

LINDA COLLINS

On his way back downstream toward the Twin Cities, Thoreau made special note of the extensive hardwood forests that he passed between the sharp bend in the river at Mankato and Fort Snelling. The dense stands of elm, basswood, maple and oak that he observed were part of what was then known as the Big Woods—a swath of deciduous forest that ran from northwest to southeast through the central part of the state.

The Big Woods were at their thickest in the very region through which Thoreau passed. And it is here that their legacy has been preserved at several parks—Sakatah Lake State Park east of Mankato and Nerstrand Woods State Park south of Northfield are two fine examples—where stands of the grand trees still can be seen. Elsewhere, however, they quickly fell victim to the axes and sawblades of settlers who were eager to clear land for farming.

Typically, when a settler established a homestead in the wilderness the first trees cleared were used to build a log house. Then, as time passed and civilization made sufficient inroads, someone would set up a sawmill and the old log dwellings slowly gave way to "stick built," or wood-frame, constructions made of hardwood species harvested from the settlers' fields.

This process has been well preserved at the Geldner Sawmill—a steam-powered mill that has been scrupulously maintained at its original obscure location a few miles southeast of the town of Cleveland on Le Sueur County Road 13. The second Sunday each month through the summer, you'll find smoke billowing out of the mill's tall stack as sawyer John Ballman and engineer John Zimmerman team up to get the big circular saw and its several accessories whirring. As they go about their labors, they take time to answer questions, and expound with considerable knowledge upon the mechanics of steam-age technology. The two bring to life the local farmers in the days when they began to depend more and more on steam power.

Just getting their horse-drawn sleds full of logs to the mill was challenge enough for people living in an area where roads were scarce and poorly maintained. As a result, most heavy hauling was done in winter on a network of "winter roads," which used the frozen surfaces of lakes wherever possible. Upon arrival at the mill, the logs would be unloaded and the sawyer's crew would go to work, employing what in 1870 was state-of-the-art equipment.

Operating with a 40-horsepower boiler and a 147-horsepower engine, the main saw was (and still is) capable

The grand trees of the Big Woods quickly fell to the axes of settlers eager to clear the land for farming.

At the Geldner Sawmill **(below)** *near Cleveland, engineer John Zimmerman* **(right)** *stokes the steam boiler and the sawdust flies one Sunday each month throughout the summer. As Zimmerman and sawyer John Ballman* **(facing page)** *explain the evolution of the machinery, the conditions under which employees worked and the lifestyles of the local farmers, a vivid picture of rural Minnesota in the mid-1800s takes shape in your imagination.*

of handling hardwood logs up to 20 feet in length. To accomplish this task, a network of thick leather belts stretched long distances between pulleys were sent into motion until the energy was finally passed on from engine to saw. This much was standard operating procedure for steam sawmills at the time. However, the Geldner mill posessed a special innovation that quadrupled productivity and reduced by half the number of workers needed to help run the saw. This was a special ratchet device on the log-supporting carriage that enabled one worker operating a single lever to move a huge log into the correct position for each pass by the blade.

While such advances in technology were slowly making their way into the thinning hardwood forests of south-central Minnesota, the nearby Minnesota River town of St. Peter was enjoying a quiet interlude between two scandals that brought considerable public attention to an otherwise pleasant but unremarkable small town.

The first of these took place in 1857, during the last year of Minnesota's status as a territory. Evidently prompted by nothing more than naked greed, the territorial governor, Willis A. Gorman, and several other legislators had conspired to carry out an ingenious plan to steal Minnesota's capital away from St. Paul and bestow it upon St. Peter, making themselves rich in the bargain. The conspirators had purchased considerable tracts of land in St. Peter, and then managed to sneak a bill through the legislature authorizing the transfer of the seat of power. Although Twin Citians were outraged when news of the bill reached the press, Governor Gorman was less than repentant. At one point during the controversy he was quoted as saying: "Remove the Capital to St. Peter and I am worth $200,000 and the State is as poor as a mouse; keep the Capital in St. Paul, the State is rich and I am poor as a mouse."

A scheme to thwart the governor and his chums that was as wild and ethically marginal as the original offence was carried out by a colorful dog-sledding, fur-trading legislator from Pembina County named Joe Rolette. Under a smokescreen created by his colleagues, Rolette is reported to have simply absconded with the bill and hidden out in the top floor of a St. Paul hotel, playing cards with his friends, until the session was over. Aided by a tactical maneuver that prevented any business from being accomplished without full attendance in the legislature, the governor's plan was foiled and Rolette enjoyed a hero's torchlight parade in St. Paul.

St. Peter, on the other hand, was accorded the dubious distinction of receiving the state's first insane asylum, the St.

"Remove the Capital to St. Peter and I am worth $200,000 and the State is as poor as a mouse..."

Peter Regional Treatment Center. Today the center houses a very interesting museum that chronicles the history of the treatment of patients with various kinds of mental disorders from the late 19th century up to the present.

The second scandal that brought another wave of notoriety to St. Peter involved one of the community's more prominent citizens—a Democratic legislator, senator and district magistrate named E. St. Julien Cox. It appears that in the course of his public career, Judge Cox offended a sufficient number of his constituents that, in 1878, they raised a public stink over certain practices that had become part of the *modus operandi* of the Cox courtroom. The charges revolved around the judge's alleged drunkenness at the bench and such etiquette as sending defendants out for a bucket of beer before being sentenced and the impromptu scheduling of concerts, featuring the judge himself on the melodeon. His

accusers even claimed that Judge Cox was not above taking an occasional snooze when the courtroom action was slow.

Cox was ousted from the bench after a spectacularly public six-month trial that resulted in a whopping 7,000 pages of testimony. Although friends in the legislature passed a resolution annulling the impeachment in 1891, Cox left the state in 1898 to live in Los Angeles. Visitors to St. Peter would do well to stop in for a visit to the E. St. Julien Cox House, at 500 Washington Street—which has been well preserved inside and out as one of Minnesota's most outstanding examples of a Gothic Revival-style dwelling and carriage house.

Some 40 miles northeast of St. Peter as the crow flies, on the other side of a region of numerous lakes, the town of Northfield is clustered along the banks of the Cannon River. Founded originally as a milling site drawing power from the

27

Northfield's Division Street is refined, cultured and sedate.

river, today the cultural influences of two excellent small liberal arts colleges—Carlton and St. Olaf—give Northfield much of its character. The beautiful French Second Empire-style Archer Hotel, built in 1877, is the hub of a cluster of small restaurants and shops along Division Street that are frequented by students, faculty and visitors. The atmosphere of this setting is refined, cultured and sedate.

However, a block south of the hotel on this main street is a museum that recaptures an event early in the town's history that was anything but sedate. For it was here, on September 7, 1876, at what was then the First National Bank of Northfield, that one of Minnesota's most famous bank robberies was thwarted by a group of gutsy citizens.

As was their fashion, the eight members of the James-Younger gang entered Northfield on that Thursday morning expecting to easily knock off the town bank. To their surprise—indeed, to their ultimate demise—the good citizens of Northfield weren't prepared to give in without a fight.

Three members of the gang—including, it is believed, Jesse James himself, entered the bank while five of the robbers occupied positions in the street outside. But their characteristic knee-length linen "dusters" gave their identities away and a couple of alert townsfolk, sensing what was happening, cried an alarm. Meanwhile, inside the bank the head cashier, Joseph Lee Heywood, refused to open the vault. The courage Heywood displayed in taking this stand cost him his life, as the robbers shot the cashier in the head when they hastily beat a retreat.

Outside, a street fight ensued that resulted in two townsfolk being killed along with two gang members. And in the weeks that followed, the capture in west-central Minnesota of all but Jesse and Frank James resulted in the final dissolution of the James-Younger gang.

The Northfield Historical Society museum has immortalized this event by reconstructing the interior of the bank to look just as it did on the day of the raid. There is also a video documentary on the episode, along with a room full of exhibits including guns, photos, contemporary press accounts and personal effects once belonging to members of the James-Younger gang—including, incredibly enough, a severed ear that once was attached to Charlie Pitts.

CONNIE WANNER

CHRIS POLYDOROFF

Left: *Northfield's Archer House Hotel is one of Minnesota's most gracious historic inns. The local press noted upon the French Second Empire–style hotel's opening in 1877 that "There is unequivocal indication of taste in every room," and the same holds true today.*
Below: *Each autumn, as many as 100,000 visitors descend upon Northfield for a re-enactment of the most famous bank robbery in Minnesota history. Jesse James and his bandits were fended off by a determined populace and a brave cashier when the James-Younger gang attempted an unauthorized withdrawal from the former First National Bank, now a museum dedicated to the episode.*

Facing page: *The civilized tastes of collegiate life are found everywhere in Northfield—from the quaint cafes and taverns in the restored town center **(right)** to the English Elizabethan buildings on the St. Olaf campus**(left).***

29

Pipestone National Monument

Blue Mounds State Park

Jeffers Petroglyphs

Lake Shetek State Park

Currie

Above: A rock carving, circa 1838, survives as a monument to cartographer Joseph Nicollet.

Facing page: The reddish-brown pipestone has been prized for centuries for Indian ceremonial pipes. Found between layers of Sioux quartzite (seen here), the softer pipestone still is quarried and used by artisans at the Pipestone National Monument interpretive center and elsewhere.

PIPESTONE & PRAIRIE GRASS

Bright, clear sky over a plain so wide that the rim of the heavens cut down on it around the entire horizon....Bright, clear sky, to-day, to-morrow, and for all time to come.

...And sun! And still more sun! It set the heavens afire every morning; it grew with the day to quivering golden light—then softened into all the shades of red and purple as evening fell....Pure colour everywhere. A gust of wind, sweeping across the plain, threw into life waves of yellow and blue and green.

Giants in the Earth
O.E. Rolvaag

Such was the appearance of the prairie of southwestern Minnesota to the earliest European-American explorers and settlers. It was an ocean of coarse, tall, beautiful grasses that ran to every horizon and beyond—an ocean with its own magnificence and special perils. There were massive herds of bison, sweeping fires that threatened to consume everything in sight, clouds of crop-eating locusts that descended from the heavens and blizzards that were so severe one could become dangerously—mortally—lost only a few feet from familiar ground.

The predominant response of the white man to this environment, as elsewhere, was to dominate it, tame it, and use its resources to nurture an expanding civilization. But for the Native Americans of the Great Plains the land suggested other purposes. And perhaps there is no better place to gain some appreciation of this fact than to visit the sacred pipestone quarries at Pipestone National Monument. This was a destination of peaceful pilgrimages made by tribal groups from all over the Great Plains, who came to quarry stone for their ceremonial pipes.

The quarry, just north of the city of Pipestone and west of Route 75, is in a shallow wooded valley dissected by meandering Pipestone Creek. Your visit to the monument begins at an interpretive center where pipestone artifacts are on display and for sale, a film is shown on the history of the quarry and, from April through October, native artisans demonstrate their craftsmanship on chunks of the reddish-brown stone. The path into the quarry begins just outside the interpretive center and disappears into the underbrush to follow the banks of the gentle stream. Between the trees and shrubs you can glimpse the surrounding walls of quartzite and pipestone that rise a dozen feet or so from the valley floor and form a rough ellipse.

In contrast, there wasn't a single tree to be found in 1838 when the French-American cartographer and astronomer Joseph N. Nicollet visited the quarries as head of the first official government expedition to the region. His travels occurred before a wealth of exotic vegetation had been introduced to the prairie and the specter of the prairie fire, which regenerated the wild grasses while killing off any competitors, had been effectively extinguished.

Nicollet's arrival in the valley was met with a response from nature that coincided with the Dakotas' vision of reality. "In the opinion of the Sioux, who are fond of the marvelous," he wrote in his journal, "this quarry was opened by the great spirit of thunder, and one cannot visit it without being greeted by his rumblings and the lightning and storms that accompany them. We are able to testify on our part of the truth of this tradition, or at least our experience accorded with it. We were not one-half mile from the valley of thunder when lightning and heavy rain burst upon us and violent winds nearly upset Mr. Renville's wagon, holding us up for several minutes before we were able to begin the short descent into the valley."

GLENN VAN NIMWEGEN

The storm quickly passed and Nicollet and his party spent several peaceful days making geographic and astronomical observations to augment his map of the Mississippi and Missouri rivers' watersheds. Nicollet also spent time with several Dakota families camped nearby and with sensitivity he recorded the practices of the men who went about preparing to quarry the stone. He noted that they fasted and purified themselves for three days, abstained from contact with the opposite sex and engaged in a ceremony of prayers and offerings to the spirit of the quarry, "so that he will let them have good stone which will not flake and is clear and compact and uniform."

At Leaping Rock, young Indian men jumped across a six-foot chasm to land atop a small pinnacle and impress the maidens.

KENT & DONNA DANNEN

LINDA COLLINS

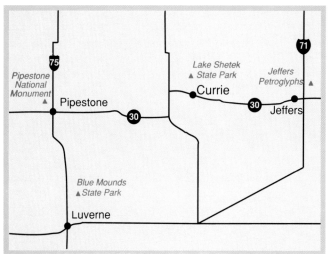

JEFF GNASS

Below: *Pipestone Creek flows over Winnewissa Falls through the center of the pipestone quarry. Prairie grasses once predominated where trees and shrubs now thrive. These exotic plant species usurped the grasses' domain with the coming of white settlers and the end of rejuvenating prairie fires.*

Facing page, left: *Native artisans use traditional chisel and hammer to free the pipestone from the surrounding Sioux quartzite at Pipestone National Monument. According to Dakota Indian tradition, men intending to work in the quarry first must undergo several days of ritual purification.*

Right: *Blue Mounds State Park, a sanctuary for Minnesota's now-rare prairie grasses, also boasts a mysterious line of boulders that many suspect played a part in ancient Indian astronomy.*

33

Nicollet wrote that the area had "ravenous beauty…This admirable hill awaits the poet and the painter, who should visit it when the last rays of the setting sun fall upon it."

Once quarried using an age-old technology of wedges and hammers, the soft red stone was fashioned into a variety of bowl shapes. Then the pipes were consecrated and joined with a straight wooden stem, at which point they were put to their frequent ceremonial uses.

Even the most casual smoking of pipes entailed significant ritual. The sharing of a pipe by a sociable gathering of men seated in a circle around the campfire in a tipi would be initiated by the host, whose customary position was opposite the door. He would light the pipe, offer smoke to the principal powers of the universe, take a puff or two and then pass the pipe to the man on his right. The pipe continued to make its way around the circle in this fashion until it came to the door of the tipi. Here it was passed back all the way around the circle to the man awaiting the pipe who then smoked and continued passing the pipe to his right.

Before leaving the quarry, Nicollet and his men took time to carve their names and the date of their visit on the

MARK E. GIBSON

34

face of a rock that is still visible today near a tall promontory called Leaping Rock. This free-standing quartzite chimney offered a challenge to young Indian men who would leap across a chasm of about a half-dozen feet to land on its small pinnacle—often, according to tradition, to win the heart of a maiden. The explorer's party put Leaping Rock to another use when, on July 4, they used it as a platform on which to erect the Stars and Stripes.

Nicollet was clearly moved both by the Dakota he met at the pipestone quarry and by the beauty of the site itself. "Nothing equals the reserve and discretion of these good people," he wrote, adding prophetically, "I cannot conceive why so many whites blunder in their dealings with them...A little tobacco and a few [kind] words will do what an army cannot do."

Of the land, he felt himself unequal to the task of describing its "ravenous beauty....This admirable hill awaits the poet and the painter, who should visit it when the last rays of the setting sun fall upon it."

Not far from this sacred quarry are two more places where the same quartzite bedrock breaks through the surface to disrupt the expanse of agricultural fields that roll onward toward all horizons. The first, at Blue Mounds State Park just north of Luverne, is even more dramatic than the protrusion of pipestone-imbedded quartzite at Pipestone. In fact, the Blue Mounds received their name from settlers traveling west, who could distinguish this ridge from a considerable distance and noticed the bluish hue of a steep escarpment (as much as 100 feet high) along the eastern flank that is lined at its base with stately oaks.

As one of Minnesota's largest remaining areas of virgin prairie grasses, the Blue Mounds are a riot of color in spring when wildflowers are in bloom. There are prickly pear cacti, too, sprouting delicate yellow flowers, large quartzite boulders and areas of exposed bedrock covered with lichens that have grown over the centuries into colorful and complex patterns. What's more, the park has been populated with a small herd of bison, which serves to complete the illusion that time truly has been reversed and you have been transported back to the prairie of 100 years ago. If you tire of watching the stoic buffalo, there is also extensive hiking on top of and below the elevated Blue Mounds, a lake for swimming, and camping and picnicking facilities.

In a more mysterious vein, near the park's southern border is a 1,200-foot-long line of stones that seem to have been placed intentionally along an axis that corresponds to

LOUIE BUNDE, UNICORN STOCK PHOTOS

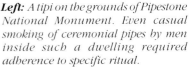

Left: A tipi on the grounds of Pipestone National Monument. Even casual smoking of ceremonial pipes by men inside such a dwelling required adherence to specific ritual.
Below: A configuration of more than 2,000 ancient rock carvings, or petroglyphs, at Jeffers Petroglyphs, represents Minnesota's largest single accumulation of such carvings. Their age, purposes and creators remain mysteries.

Facing page, top: A resident herd of American bison (buffalo) wanders the prairie of Blue Mounds State Park.
Bottom: The waters of Pipestone Creek momentarily pool downstream of Winnewissa Falls.

GEORGE HULSTRAND, JR.

the alignment of the rising and setting sun at the fall and spring equinoxes. Much controversy exists concerning who may have been responsible for hauling these stones into their present position. Exactly what purpose this effort may have served is a further enigma.

The third well known outcropping of quartzite bedrock in the region is more cryptic still. This site, known as the Jeffers Petroglyphs, is found a few miles east of Jeffers and just north of Minnesota Highway 30. A dome of quartzite pokes through the surface here to form a small ridge. On its polished surface, unidentified prehistoric artists took great pains to chisel almost 2,000 rock carvings that are preserved today by the Minnesota Historical Society as a gallery of a long-extinct prairie culture.

I visited the petroglyphs on a sunny spring afternoon and set out on the quarter-mile interpretive trail leading from a tipi-shaped shelter staffed by Minnesota Historical Society personnel. The top of the ridge provided a lovely view of the prairie in all directions, and bunches of wildflowers and flitting birds brought to life in a special way the prairie grasses that surrounded the carvings. It seemed like an inspiring enough place to give rise to the creative impulse— although the carvings at my feet seemed to have demanded of the artist more than just a flirting interest in putting ideas or representations into stone. Each carving, I learned from the staff at the site, was slowly chipped into the hard quartzite by means of a pointed rock held in the fist that was struck with a hammerstone.

Many of the carvings are clearly representational. There are animals—bison, bear, wolf, turtle, elk—and people in the form of stick figures wielding spears, bows and arrows, or wearing head-dresses reminiscent of those used by Dakota medicine men in historic times. There are representations of hands and footprints, too. And there are many other carvings that are abstract enough to defy easy recognition.

It was a most peaceful place to visit. I returned to my car reminded that the natural prairies and their inhabitants coexisted such a long, long time before the coming of the white man. I felt some yearning again to have known the land before it was transformed into its present state—an occurrence that, in the grand scheme of things, happened just yesterday.

What else to do in Prairieland? First, for accommodations you may want to reserve a room at the Calumet Hotel in Pipestone—a handsome late-19th century stone structure that has been tastefully renovated and appointed with period

TOM TILL

antiques and antique reproductions. A respectable restaurant and pub are found at entry level.

In addition to the wonderful expanses of prairie at Blue Mounds State Park, there is another state park in the area that provides an interesting historical lesson and plentiful water-oriented recreational opportunities. Lake Shetek State Park, two miles north of Currie on Murray County Road 37, is in the center of a heavily wooded area known as the Great Oasis because of its numerous small lakes and ponds and the larger Lake Shetek. This is one of the places in the region that was a site of a bloody clash between white settlers and Dakota warriors in the Dakota conflict of 1862 (see next chapter for information on the conflict). Park interpretive naturalists offer an annual program in August, "Shetek Revisited," to acquaint visitors with the events that led to the killing of 11 settlers and several Indians at Slaughter Slough.

Not far away in Currie there's a wonderful museum dedicated to the history of the railroad and the role it once played in connecting the inhabitants of small rural Minnesota towns to the rest of the world. When the train arrived in Currie, located at the end of a spur line, the engine needed some means of getting turned around for the return trip. The solution was a turntable—a piece of track balanced on a pivot upon which an engine and coal car could be swung around 180 degrees by the muscle power of a single lineman. This simple and formerly common device, which is now one of only two in the state, may still inspire a bit of wonder at the accomplishments of human ingenuity.

Inside the old railroad shed at the museum, which used to house locomotives, is an interesting collection of railroad equipment and memorabilia. Included here is a delightful vehicle, used by track and telegraph-line workers, called a velocipede—an odd-looking, three-wheeled bicycle-like contraption that reached speeds of 20 miles per hour by means of a two-handled push-pull stick.

The restored depot next door has been renovated to look much as it once did, complete with waiting rooms segregated by sex. This arrangement was popular until the 1920s, at which time men apparently either grew less concerned about being in the company of the opposite sex while indulging in such vile habits as spitting tobacco, or women decided they could tolerate the presence of their uncouth partners. Also, in the old baggage room there is an excellent scale model of the depot and railroad yards as they appeared in the 1940s.

Below: *Lake Shetek and the surrounding Lake Shetek State Park are in the center of what is known locally as the Great Oasis—a lovely hardwood grove surrounded by a network of lakes amidst the dominance of farm and prairie. Historic sites in the park include this preserved pioneer cabin and monuments to a tragic event of the Dakota Conflict of 1862.*

Facing page: *Occasional areas of virgin prairie grass, such as this one at Pipestone, suggest how the land appeared before the onslaught of the plow.*

CONNIE WANNER

New Ulm
Harkin Store
Redwood Falls
Lac Qui Parle Mission
Forest City
Acton
Fort Ridgely
Birch Coulee
Lower Sioux Agency

Above: Markers throughout the Minnesota River valley commemorate the deaths of white settlers and soldiers during the bloody Dakota conflict of 1862. The Indian side of the story is left largely untold.
Facing page: Lac Qui Parle Mission on the Minnesota, a reminder of peaceful days.

THE RIVER OF CONFLICT

The valley of the Minnesota River from its elbow at Mankato upstream to Montevideo brings a sudden and welcome change to the prairie landscape. The gentle bluffs of the valley and the floodplain are lush with tall hardwoods. Lazy river currents flow through the heart of this long green oasis, affording a pleasant relief from the expanse of agricultural lands that roll oceanlike to either horizon.

The towns that have sprouted along this section of the Minnesota are appealing too. There's New Ulm—a tidy community of 13,000 that has been fiercely proud of its solid German heritage since settlement times in the mid-19th century. The historic Schell Brewery and its gardens and mansion, which are open for summer tours, are splendid survivals of Old Country family brewing tradition. And New Ulm's well endowed Brown County Historical Museum must be the only museum in the state that has exhibit labels posted in both English and German.

Not far upstream from New Ulm on the other side of the river is a wonderfully preserved general store that whisks visitors back to the turn of the century. When business at the Harkin Store was finally undermined by the routing of the railroad farther south, its doors were closed with most merchandise left intact. Today about 40 percent of the items on the shelves and hanging on the walls of the store are original—although you would have a difficult time pointing out anything inauthentic. Even the worn wooden pieces on the checkerboard that rests on a wooden barrel beside the wood stove are the real McCoy.

Redwood Falls, another 30 miles upriver, surrounds the state's largest and most alluring municipal park, named Alexander Ramsey Park after Minnesota Territory's first governor. A zoo, extensive exercise and hiking trails, sites for camping and fishing, and an inspiring waterfall hidden in a deep ravine all are found here amidst 217 rugged bluff-land acres.

Several other hospitable, wholesome little communities—like Granite Falls and Montevideo—have tastefully accommodated their growth to the shady banks of the Minnesota. And there are four state parks in the valley, too, providing visitors opportunities to hike, camp, picnic, canoe, ski, snowmobile and golf.

The oldest historic site in the valley harking back to the pre-settlement era has been preserved as a memorial of a peaceful time when relatively good relations prevailed between white traders, missionaries and local bands of Dakota Indians. The Lac Qui Parle mission, founded in 1835, is on the banks of the Minnesota where Chippewa County Road 13 crosses the river. A reconstructed church stands today where once there were a half-dozen other buildings, including a school and residences for the missionaries. It was here that the Bible was first translated into the Dakota language, via a written alphabet developed by the missionaries.

But amidst all this pastoral serenity are many public reminders that life has not always been so peaceful up and down the Minnesota and upon the surrounding prairie. For six weeks in the late summer and early fall of 1862—while the rest of the nation was preoccupied with what appeared to be a likely Rebel victory in the Civil War—this region was the site of one of America's most tragic and brutal wars between Indians and whites.

It is possible to piece together the events of the Dakota conflict of 1862 by visiting and studying the many landmarks and historic sites that note locations of battles, ambushes and ugly encounters between the Santee Dakota and the white soldiers and settlers. As I undertook this pilgrimage to the

Although his warehouse was filled with food for them, agent Thomas Galbraith made the Dakota go hungry.

CONNIE WANNER

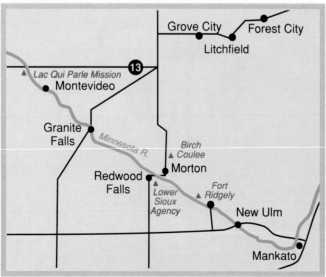

LINDA COLLINS

official shrines of Minnesota history, however, it quickly became apparent that the story was incomplete.

This notion first occurred to me upon visiting a reconstruction of a stockade erected hastily by panicked settlers near the little town of Forest City, north of the Minnesota River in Meeker County. The stockade is a crude shelter consisting of a small palisade of rough-hewn pine logs surrounding a one-room log building. It has a large front gate, and observation towers mounted in all four corners of the compound provide views of the encircling fields.

Within these walls more than 240 men, women and children spent some 10 days crouched in fear of an attack that never came. Their apprehensions were fueled by the murder of a white family in nearby Acton by four young Santee Dakota men—the event that triggered the ensuing conflict.

Upon hearing the news of the "Acton massacre," one family was so anxious to reach the safety of the stockade that the parents abandoned their 13-year-old daughter, who was working the distant fields, leaving her a note with instructions to find her own way to the stockade (which she managed to do). It was through anecdotes like this one, shared by the volunteer staff at the site, that I was able to generate some picture of who occupied the cramped stockade and what their fears and experiences were like. The Dakota, however, remained anonymous—their motives ambiguous and their experiences unaccounted for.

A state historical marker titled "The Acton Incident" near Grove City explains the killings that took place there as follows: "On a bright Sunday afternoon, August 17, 1862, four young Sioux hunters, on a spur-of-the-moment dare, decided to prove their bravery by shooting Robinson Jones, the postmaster and storekeeper at Acton...." Until I came across the long silent voices of the Dakota themselves, who much later related their story to a historian, I was shocked by the idea that the murder of a man and his family could be undertaken as casually and recklessly as the marker suggested. As I eventually learned, though the four Sioux were indeed brutal, the circumstances under which they were living at the time cast a different light on the Acton incident and the entire "Sioux Uprising."

Having reluctantly agreed to give up their nomadic way of life and their hunting grounds through the signing of several dubious treaties, all 7,000 of the Santee Dakota had been confined, since 1851, to two small reservations along the southern banks of the Minnesota—an area equal to one

tenth of their former lands. Here they were supposed to learn to farm under the direction of white government agents and their staff. By the summer of 1862, however, many of the Indians were facing starvation due to crop failure, drought and exhausted hunting resources on their shrunken lands.

The Indian agent at the Lower Sioux Agency near Redwood Falls, Thomas Galbraith, insisted on awaiting the arrival of tardy annuity payments from Washington before providing the Dakota with access to a warehouse full of food destined for them. Santee Dakota Chief Little Crow's urgent request of Galbraith on August 15 to make special arrangements to provide his people with food was met with this response from trader Andrew Myrick, who spoke on the agent's behalf: "If they are hungry let them eat grass or their own dung."

Big Eagle, another Dakota chief, described what happened in the encounter with the settlers at Acton two days later: Four young men from Shakopee's band came across a hen and some eggs inside the fence of a settler's farm. One of the men picked up the eggs, intending to take them. But,

Below: *Each summer, mountain men, voyageurs and other historic characters rendezvous at the Forest City Stockade, a shelter to settlers in 1862.*

Left, top and bottom: *Visitors to the Harkin store step back in time to the turn of the century, when this general store shut down with its shelves stocked full of dry goods, miraculous tonics, and almost anything else an enterprising farm family might have required.*

Facing page: *Schell Brewery in New Ulm, which survived the Dakota conflict of 1862 with loss of only two and a half barrels of beer, still produces a variety of fine malt beverages.*

Right: *The Minnesota River wends its way through Granite Falls, a peaceful town that was the home of the father of prohibition, Congressman Andrew Volstead. Just outside town is some of the oldest exposed rock on the face of the earth—Morton gneiss, formed more than 3 billion years ago.*

Facing page: *The site, at Lower Sioux Agency, where the 1862 trial of 392 Dakota resulted in death sentences for 303 of the defendants.*

R. HAMILTON SMITH

COURT MARTIAL SITE

although they were half-starved, the young men fell into disagreement as to whether or not they should steal eggs that belonged to a white man. The most reluctant among them was called a coward by the one who had taken the eggs, and he responded to this grave insult by saying, according to Dee Brown in *Bury My Heart at Wounded Knee*, "I am not a coward. I am not afraid of the white man, and to show you that I am not I will go to the house and shoot him." There were other whites at the settlement too, and in the end three men and two women were murdered. The Sioux returned to their camp and reported what had happened to their elders.

Little Crow, the tribal leader with the greatest following and the recognized war chief, rebuked the attackers—who with their peers were anxious to make war on all the whites in the valley and drive them away—knowing that retribution for their actions that day would be swift and severe. But Little Crow had been to Washington and had seen the extensive armies of the whites. He counseled restraint, but the younger warriors had no patience for such talk. Sensing that his attempts to dissuade them from fighting were futile, Little Crow, as his son recalled, said:

"You are fools. You cannot see the face of your chief; your eyes are full of smoke. You cannot hear his voice; your ears are full of roaring waters....you are little children—you are fools. You will die like the rabbits when the hungry wolves hunt them in the Hard Moon of January."

Still, Little Crow was a warrior and a leader. And when the men accused him of being a coward, he committed himself to battle by replying, "Ta-oya-te-duta [Little Crow] is not a coward; he will die with you."

Lack of unity among the Dakota continued to undermine Little Crow and the other chiefs as they carried out a series of assaults on the Lower Sioux Agency, New Ulm and Fort Ridgely—the military garrison near New Ulm that was responsible for controlling the Indians on their reservations. Instead of presenting the white enemy with a united front, small groups of undisciplined young marauders set off on their own to raid isolated settlements outside the Minnesota valley. These raids frequently resulted in the brutal killings of entire families, while the warriors fighting under Little Crow engaged only soldiers and armed civilians.

There was also dissension among Little Crow's followers. The chief's plan to strike Fort Ridgely swiftly and drive the soldiers out of the region was overruled by the younger warriors who wanted to attack the less well-defended New Ulm. Ultimately this strategy worked against the Dakota, who found the citizens of New Ulm fully determined and capable of defending their city while the ill-prepared soldiers at Fort Ridgely used the extra time to secure badly-needed reinforcements. Two attacks against New Ulm by 100 and 650 Indians on August 19 and 21, respectively, resulted in nearly 200 buildings burned and in more than 100 white casualties—but still the Dakota were driven back.

The town has commemorated the event with an imposing granite monument to the conflict, on which the names of those who died defending their community are inscribed. The names and numbers of Dakota warriors and the extent of their casualties all go unmentioned. History has identified the enemy and left him faceless, has sung praises for those who resisted his aggressions.

The two battles at Fort Ridgely were even less successful for the Indians. A force of 800 warriors was repeatedly turned back by only 150 soldiers due to the stalwartness of the stone fort and to the effective use of cannon by the blue-coats, who loaded their artillery with canistershot (small balls that dissipated once fired, like shot from a shotgun).

Today the only building that remains standing at the fort, the Commissary, is a museum dedicated to the preservation of the lifestyles of the men who so successfully defended their garrison. A tall granite obelisk at the center of the Fort Ridgely grounds, surrounded by the foundations of a dozen other buildings, recognizes each soldier and citizen who fought in the battles on August 21 and 23. The soldiers lost three men in the fighting; Dakota losses were estimated to

Chief Little Crow wanted to attack Fort Ridgely, but younger warriors insisted on New Ulm.

43

Right: The partially reconstructed Fort Ridgely, at Fort Ridgely State Park, occupies a prominent site on a bluff-top field that is surrounded by steep ravines—the site of two days of fighting between soldiers and Dakota in August 1862. The restored commissary building now houses excellent exhibits on the history of the fort, the Dakota conflict and on military life in the 1860s.

Facing page: A Dakota burial mound at Granite Falls across from Upper Sioux Agency.

have been much greater, although, as usual, went unrecorded.

I visited the battlefield at Birch Coulee near the little town of Morton one clear spring morning, when the dew-damp prairie wild flowers were in bloom and the air was filled with the chatter of song birds. It was an open field of several acres with two parallel lines of tall trees running the length of its middle. Here on the early morning of September 5, Big Eagle's and Mankato's warriors quietly surrounded an encampment of soldiers. "Just at dawn the fight began," Big Eagle later recalled (recounted in *Bury My Heart at Wounded*

Knee). "It continued all day and the following night until late the next morning. Both sides fought well. Owing to the white men's way of fighting they lost many men. Owing to the Indians' way of fighting they lost but few...."

Facing a nearby highway was a stone and metal marker:

Battle of Birch Coulee
On the prairie half a mile east of this point a party of about 160 troops was attacked by Sioux at dawn, Sept. 2, 1862.
During the battle, the force was surrounded for thirty hours, losing over a third of its number in killed and wounded.

And on the northern outskirts of Morton a monument added this touch to posterity: "Erected by the State of Minnesota in grateful remembrance of the Heroism of those gallant soldiers and citizens who fought the battle of Birch Coulee and to perpetuate their names." A list followed of the names of all whites who engaged in the battle, punctuated by an occasional "wounded" or "killed." No mention of Dakota losses was made.

But perhaps there is some justice in this state of affairs after all, even if it be only poetic. For, in this small and ultimately insignificant battle, the Santee Dakota prevailed. Fighting to preserve a way of life and a culture that has been as successfully extinguished as the once-ubiquitous prairie grasses have been rent and turned under by the plow, Big Eagle and Mankato knew a moment of victory. And the field of grasses and flowers—a scarred and embattled one at that—speaks as loudly in its own way as the enduring, if lifeless, stone and metal monuments left by the whites.

A few hundred yards from the edge of the battlefield, the elevated bluff gives way to a lovely view of the Minnesota valley and the town of Morton down below. From this viewpoint I could see outcroppings of the oldest exposed rock on the face of the earth—a distinguished lichen-covered gray and pink granite called Morton gneiss (pronounced "nice"). Not far out of sight across the river on Dakota land was the site of the Lower Sioux Agency, where Indian agent Thomas Galbraith had turned his back on a disenfranchised and desperate people.

The evening before I had visited what remains of the Lower Sioux Agency—a reconstructed stone warehouse, a scattering of historic markers noting where other buildings once stood and a modern interpretive center that is managed by the Minnesota Historical Society and dedicated to preserving some taste of the cultural history of the Minnesota

CONNIE WANNER PHOTOS BOTH PAGES

Right: *Members of the New Ulm Battery join craftsmen, fur traders and others in bringing the late 1800s to life at the annual Fort Ridgely Historical Festival.*

Facing page: *This waterfall is a central attraction at Alexander Ramsey Park in Redwood Falls—the largest municipal park in the state.*

Santee Dakota. By then, having visited so many sites related to the conflict where the presence of the Dakota had been reduced to little more than an amorphous but savage force, I welcomed the opportunity to gain some perspective on who the Dakota once were and how they lived.

Exhibits at the center retrace the Dakotas' story from the present back more than 200 years, when they were pushed by their traditional enemies, the Ojibway, out onto the prairie from the woodlands of Minnesota and Wisconsin. As the tale unfolded, I was especially struck by the richness and tenacity of Dakota culture, by its strong spiritual grounding and its harmonious relationship to the natural environment.

The exhibits also reveal how the conclusion of the 1862 conflict virtually sounded the death knell to the Dakota way of life in Minnesota. Having lost the critical battles at Fort Ridgely and New Ulm, it was only a matter of time before the Indians admitted defeat. And those who chose to surrender instead of fleeing to the unoccupied plains to the west or into Canada were either deported to reservations in North and South Dakota or taken as prisoners to await trial and execution. There were 303 warriors in the latter category, tried by court martial at Lower Sioux Agency, all of whom were sentenced to be hanged.

After passing responsibility for approving these executions on to President Lincoln, Colonel Henry Hastings Sibley and others were shocked to learn that Lincoln had pardoned all but 39 of the Santee Dakota for lack of conclusive evidence. Still, the mass execution that took place in Mankato on the day after Christmas, 1862, was the largest ever held in this country. And as the 38 warriors were dropped to their deaths through the gallows (a last-minute reprieve spared one warrior), the Dakota way of life in western Minnesota effectively came to an end. The remaining 1,700 prisoners spent a horrible winter locked up in a compound in the shadow of Fort Snelling awaiting their relocation to reservations in the North and South Dakota. Until the 1880s, when a few Dakota moved back to the Minnesota Valley, the entire area was virtually devoid of its original inhabitants. Today the few Indians living near the Lower Sioux Agency are all that remains here of what was once a thriving people.

**Sauk Centre
Sinclair Lewis Home
Charles Lindbergh
Home
Minnesota Military
Museum
Living Memorial
Forest
St. John's University
Abbey and Church**

Above: The largest stained glass window in the world graces the north wall of St. John's University Church.
Facing page: Sauk Centre was the boyhood home and a source of inspiration for Nobel Prize–winning author Sinclair Lewis.

HEARTLAND TOUR

If Minnesota's heartland doesn't bowl you over upon your first encounter, don't be surprised—but don't believe what you see either. True, the area is fairly flat, largely agricultural, and apparently lacking in any special attributes that might distinguish it from many other large tracts of plowed-under Midwestern prairie or cleared hardwood forest.

But there are two things about the heartland that you wouldn't suspect on the basis of a quick once-over. The first is that, despite appearances, there are indeed a number of unusual attractions that draw visitors from all over the country and even abroad. Also, two of America's most famous 20th century personages spent their formative years here. And if Charles Lindbergh Jr. and Sinclair Lewis were sufficiently nourished by the expanses of open land to launch their stellar careers, perhaps there's more going on than meets the eye.

Lewis spent what biographers have called an "unhappy boyhood" in the town of Sauk Centre collecting the experiences that formed the basis for his world-famous fiction about life in small town America. His most renowned book, *Main Street*, published in 1920 and partly responsible for his winning America's first Nobel Prize in literature, told the tale of Carol Kennicott. A hopeful, cultured young woman from Minneapolis, she marries a doctor and comes with him to live in his home town, Gopher Prairie.

She hates it there. The people are devoid of curiosity and refinement and the environment they have built for themselves is graceless and unnurturing. The "thick voices bellowing pidgin German or trolling out dirty songs" from inside a "fly-buzzing saloon," for example, suggest to her "the delicacy of a mining-camp minus its vigor." Not far away is the "Minniemashie House" hotel: "It was a tall lean shabby structure....In the hotel office she could see a stretch of bare unclean floor. The dining room beyond was a jungle of stained tablecloths and catsup bottles."

But for all the disdain expressed by Carol of her new prairie home—and for all the outrage generated by Lewis' critical treatment of his fictionalized Sauk Centre—Lewis remained attached to his home throughout an unsettled life that took him from Minnesota to New England to Europe and, finally, back home again (he is buried in the cemetery east of town). He once wrote, "I am quite certain that I could have been born in no place in the world where I would have had more friendliness...[nor] half the fun which I had as a kid....It was a good time, a good place, and a good preparation for life."

The folk of Sauk Centre have mellowed in their views toward their prodigal son over the years too. What once was Third Avenue has been rechristened Sinclair Lewis Avenue, and Main Street is now The Original Main Street. There are large highway signs on Interstate 94 directing travelers to the Sinclair Lewis Interpretive Center—which doubles as a freeway rest-stop and Chamber of Commerce office—and the Sinclair Lewis Boyhood Home. The latter has been restored as closely as possible to the way it appeared when Lewis was a boy and is listed along with the Palmer House Hotel (which differs in appearance not much from the Minniemashie House) on the National Register of Historic Places.

No more than 40 miles from Sauk Centre is the site where Charles Lindbergh spent the first years of his life on earth (that is, before he took up flying). His parents' farm, built by his Swedish grandfather in 1901 upon leaving the old country and a powerful position in its Parliament, was in a lovely wooded grove along the banks of the Mississippi River

49

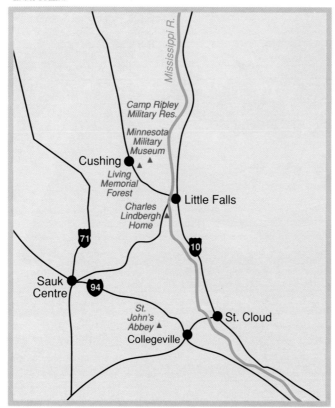

Once landed in a glaring limelight—the intensity of which Lindbergh disliked from the start—this reserved Swede from Minnesota undertook a remarkable range of pursuits. Often in the company of his wife, Anne, he continued to pioneer advances in aviation, charting many new air routes all over the world. He became interested in medical technology and helped design a breakthrough research device that keeps animal hearts alive outside the body. Lindy was very much a man of action and not especially bookish, yet he won the Pulitzer Prize for his autobiographical work, *The Spirit of St. Louis*, published in 1953.

Never one to eschew controversy, Lindbergh was very concerned about the environment and championed the protection of many endangered species. He also was outspoken on American foreign policy issues and, up until the bombing of Pearl Harbor, took a very public and highly unpopular stand against America's involvement in World War II. Once the U.S. was in the war, however, he did his part by flying in numerous combat missions.

As he grew older, Lindbergh developed an ever greater sensitivity to and appreciation of life's more mystical dimensions. The horrific use of air power in World War II and the advent of nuclear weapons tempered Lindy's enthusiasm for the technological advances that enabled him to make history in the *Spirit of St. Louis*. And at the dedication of Little Falls' Charles A. Lindbergh State Park in honor of Lindy's father in 1974, the aviation hero pronounced that the establishment of this park represented civilization's greatest achievement: the valuing of life itself over the advances of science.

To learn more about Lindbergh's fascinating life and times—he died in his adopted home of Hawaii in 1974—a visit to the Lindbergh House History Center is a must. It is located at the entrance to the state park on Minnesota 238 just south of Little Falls. The interpretive center chronicles the lives of three generations of Lindberghs, details the flight of the *Spirit of St. Louis,* and provides insights into Lindy's remarkable character by tracking his many other accomplishments.

If Charles A. Lindbergh State Park stands for civilization's greatest achievement, the Minnesota Military Museum—found about a dozen miles to the north on Minnesota 371—represents what Lindy surely would have regarded as humankind's lowest accomplishment. Still, this museum's well presented story of Minnesota's participation in armed conflict is most worthy of a visit—in part, simply because of where it is.

near Little Falls. And Lindbergh, while his interests were drawn heavenward early on, nevertheless relished romping about the woods and fields and playing in the river. It was an idyllic beginning to what was to be a most remarkable and challenge-filled life.

So many of the various things that Lindbergh undertook and so many of his experiences were extraordinary—often in ways that neither he nor anyone else would have predicted—that his life seems big enough to have filled the lives of several ordinary people. His instant rise to international fame upon completing his solo flight from New York to Paris in May 1927, for example, was something that he in no way anticipated. Before landing the *Spirit of St. Louis* in front of a hysterical crowd of 100,000—at which point he was whisked away to the American embassy—he was worried about his lack of a French visa and wondered where he could find a reasonable hotel for the night.

CONNIE WANNER PHOTOS

The military museum is on the grounds of the largest National Guard training site in the country—53,000-acre Camp Ripley. This huge military reservation derives its name from the original Fort Ripley, which was built in 1849 along the banks of the Mississippi River five miles distant in order to pacify warring Ojibway and Dakota groups.

Exhibits in the museum are divided into two sections. In one wing are displays with well selected and presented artifacts, photos, recruitment posters and documentation that recount the experiences of Minnesotans in every war since Minnesota statehood in 1858. Detailed replicas of early frontier forts are also there under glass for your review. Items that help bring to life the experiences of American and enemy soldiers in past wars include a Japanese "body flag"—a flag of the Rising Sun that was signed by a pilot's relatives and worn into battle inside the flight suit—and a table napkin

monogrammed "AH" that was taken as booty from one of Hitler's residences by a Minnesota soldier.

In a second wing at the museum there are displays of firearms as they have evolved through time. And, near the rows of machine guns, muskets and mortars, is a display dedicated to the career of a famous ex-Camp Ripley National Guardsman, John W. Vessey, who was chairman of the Joint Chiefs of Staff under President Reagan from 1982 to 1985.

The exhibits at the Minnesota Military Museum provide a glimpse into the experience of war for Minnesota soldiers that is accurate as far as it goes, but it is a decidedly dispassionate one. The mannequins that display historic

American and foreign uniforms aren't maimed or damaged for life and don't have much to say about what it's like to be a survivor of a battle in which all of one's comrades are brutally slain before one's very eyes. Ironically, to get a sense of this dimension of battle you need only take a short detour to the Living Memorial Forest a few miles west of Camp Ripley near the small town of Cushing on Route 10.

Actually, the forest itself—a somewhat random scattering of 35,000 trees in an area of rolling fields and forest that was planted by a single dedicated Vietnam vet—isn't a lot to see. But the guided tour by Geoff Steiner, the originator and maintainer of the memorial, is bound to be a powerful experience. You'll probably find Geoff where I did, in his office and house located in what used to be Cushing's post office at 5 Front Street. In this humble and cluttered space, amid boxes of American flags that Geoff sells to help make ends meet, he began to spin out for me in a somewhat rambling narrative his own remarkable story.

Geoff was a Marine who, like many others, survived the Vietnam War with serious injuries. Some were physical—he suffered facial wounds when blown off a tank by a rocket during the 1968 Tet Offensive—but the most damaging were mental and spiritual. His battle experience included witnessing the slaughter of every man in his company during the battle in which he was wounded. As a result of such trauma, Geoff returned home a changed man.

"I was a P.O.W. in my own body and in my own country," he said, and then described his years of struggle with alcoholism and severe depression, which together destroyed his first marriage. His life deteriorated to the point where he finally moved into the woods to be alone. One day in 1980, deep in despair while planting trees at his homestead, he had the inspiration of starting a memorial forest in dedication to the soldiers who were dead and missing from the war in Vietnam, and he described that moment as being a turning point in what has turned into a remarkable life.

Geoff's single-handed dedication to establishing his memorial has attracted national attention. He was featured in *Newsweek, People* and *Reader's Digest* magazines; he has been a guest at the Reagan White House and he has been acknowledged for his efforts by a number of veterans groups. He has married again and cites a newfound faith in God as a source of strength that continues to carry him toward his goal of developing a multimillion-dollar national healing center for veterans near the site of his forest. The project is an ambitious one, but given the several unpredict-

Moving along from the Minnesota Military Museum to the Living Memorial Forest gives two very different views of war.

able turns his life has taken so far, who's to say what Geoff may create in the midst of Minnesota's heartland?

Before leaving the area, a visit is in order to St. John's University Abbey and Church near Interstate 94, about 20 miles west of St. Cloud. This architectural marvel lets its presence be known to approaching travelers long before they reach the beautiful 2,400-acre wooded campus. The church's huge concrete bell banner—a great wedgelike structure with an oaken cross in its center above a line of sizable bells—can be seen rising above the tree tops against a hillside. This 2,500-ton creation is held high above the entrance to the church for all the world to see by four

gracefully sweeping legs, also made of steel-reinforced cement.

And then there's the church itself. Conceived in 1961 by architect Marcel Breuer, an orthodox Jew, whose design was selected from among 15 submissions by some of the most renowned architects in the world, the church is a grand symbol of the simple and joyous community spirit maintained by the members of St. John's Benedictine order. The building is spacious and open, with the altar in its center beneath a canopy and a series of amber skylights. Turning around to face the entry upon having entered the nave, be ready for a bit of a shock, for you'll find yourself bathed in light pouring in from

Right and facing page: The architecture of St. John's Abbey and University Church in Collegeville is so striking that for the first 10 years following its completion in 1961, this rural religious community drew more visitors than did the state capitol. Surrounding the church with its huge stained glass window and imposing bell banner are 2,400 wooded acres, which serve as a wildlife sanctuary and a wonderful place to go for a stroll.

CONNIE WANNER

GEORGE HULSTRAND, JR.

St. John's University Abbey and Church welcomes visitors to admire its architecture and enjoy the quiet of its wooded trails.

CONNIE WANNER

the north wall where the largest stained glass window in the world awaits you.

The window celebrates the seasons of the liturgical year with corresponding brilliant vertical bands of colored glass cut to various geometrical shapes. And in the center, high above this stunning sea of color, is a unifying image of God expressed through a series of roughly concentric circles. This creation was designed by a member of the St. John's University art faculty, Branislaw Bak.

Once your self-guided tour of the church is complete, you may want to hike on the abbey's extensive and not very well marked trail system that winds through thick hardwood forest and along the shores of a beautiful lake. The monks welcome you to enjoy the grounds as long as you keep in mind that this wooded retreat has been designated as a wildlife area—hence no pets or fires are allowed.

Alexandria
Moorhead
Steam Threshers'
Reunion
Inspiration Peak

Above: *The Kensington runestone has generated ample controversy and interest in Viking history since its discovery in 1898. The runic script describes the activities of a group of Viking visitors to west-central Minnesota in 1362.*

Facing page: *One of the pinnacles in Minnesota's less-than-alpine landscape is Inspiration Peak—a hillock, elevation 1,750 feet, in Otter Tail County that offers great views of the surrounding farms and woodlands.*

LAND OF THE VIKINGS

In 1354, Magnus Erickson, the ruler of Norway and Sweden, sent an expedition led by Baron Paul Knutson to the King's colony in Greenland to ensure that the colonists were remaining faithful to the Catholic Church. Some 553 years later, in 1898, a Swedish farmer named Olaf Ohman claimed to have discovered a large flat stone with a lengthy runic inscription entwined in the roots of an old tree on his farm near Kensington in Douglas County, Minnesota. Controversy has raged ever since concerning the possible connection, if any, between these two events.

The Kensington Runestone, as the 200-pound object became known, was eventually translated as describing the activities of a group of Vikings "on an exploration journey from Vinland [the eastern seaboard] westward" in the year 1362. The most complete scenario developed to bridge the rather large gap—between Magnus Erickson dispatching an expedition to Greenland and the presence of Vikings eight years later in what was to become Minnesota—was spun out in the early part of this century by Viking historian Hjalmar Holand. He devoted much of his time championing the stone's legitimacy from 1907, when he acquired the Runestone from Ohman, to his death in 1963.

Holand's idea was that the Knutson expedition found the Greenland colony abandoned and so proceeded to the North American mainland to find out what had become of the colonists. The expedition wandered about for several years, eventually following the Hudson Strait to Hudson Bay, where part of the group was thought to have followed the Nelson River to Lake Winnepeg and into Minnesota via the Red River of the North. Speculating that the group never rejoined their comrades, Holand suggested that they intermarried with the Mandan Indians of the Great Plains, thus accounting for the fair features of these natives.

There are those—including some residents of the Douglas County seat of Alexandria—who are certain beyond all doubt that the Runestone is conclusive evidence that Viking exploration of the New World pre-dated Columbus's voyage by more than 100 years. This conviction has even led the Alexandria Chamber of Commerce to place the rather bold slogan, "Alexandria/Birthplace of America," quite prominently on the shield of a much-larger-than-life and slightly cross-eyed Viking statue, which dominates North Broadway in the middle of town. Across the street from this character is the Runestone Museum, where the stone is on display along with a variety of other exhibits on Douglas County history.

On the other hand, there are the legions of historians and academicians who almost unanimously have declared the stone to be a hoax perpetrated by farmer Ohman, perhaps with some assistance from a minister friend, both of whom were well schooled in Viking lore and known for being possessed of a good sense of humor. There have been moments—such as when the Smithsonian Institution gave space for the stone in an exhibit in 1948, which prompted some sympathetic coverage by the *National Geographic* magazine—when the Runestone and Alexandria have enjoyed a certain notoriety. But, all things considered, the Kensington Runestone has perpetuated more interest in Viking tradition throughout the region then scientific support.

Surely the likelihood of a man pursuing such a dream as building a full-scale Viking ship and sailing it from Duluth to Norway would have been remote were it not for the Runestone's influence. And it was just this dream that motivated a teacher named Robert Asp from Hawley, just east of Moorhead, to begin building a full-scale, authentic

JOHN G. SHEPARD

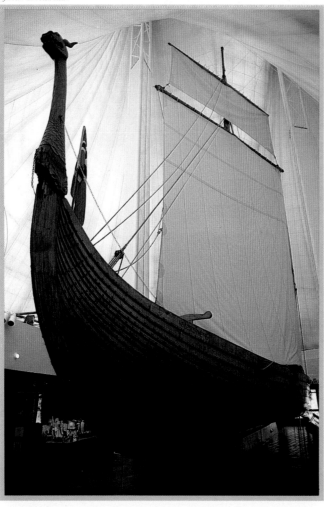

Builder Asp devoted the final years of his life to the Hjemkomst, *and was aboard for its first trial run in Duluth harbor.*

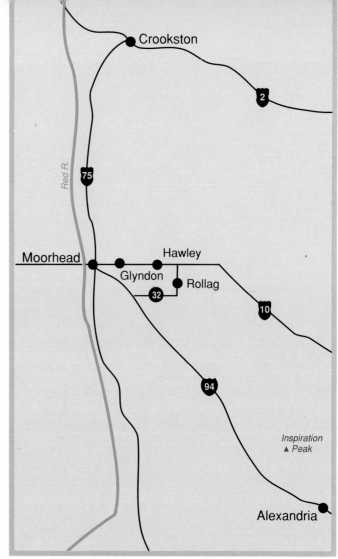

LINDA COLLINS

Viking sailing ship in 1971. The project was the central focus of the last nine years of Asp's life, at the end of which, while dying of leukemia, the ship builder was able to be on board the *Hjemkomst* (pronounced "yemkomst" and translated as "homecoming") as it set out on its first trial run in Duluth harbor.

Picking up the banner upon Asp's death, several family members joined forces with some Norwegian sailors. This enthusiastic crew successfully guided the ship across half of North America and across the Atlantic Ocean, arriving in Bergen, Norway, on July 19, 1982.

Today the good ship *Hjemkomst* is preserved for all to see at the fabulous Heritage Hjemkomst Interpretive Center, located along the banks of the Red River of the North in Moorhead. Not only is the ship itself on display in all its glory, there are exhibits about nearly every aspect of the *Hjemkomst's* construction and a high-quality documentary of the entire experience, from the design of the ship to the exuberant landing in Bergen. Generous exhibit space elsewhere in the multimillion-dollar building showcases traveling exhibitions and displays from the permanent collection of the Clay County Historical Museum.

A Viking ship, as an object of fascination, harks back to a time so far lost in the mists of history that it's relatively easy to set the imagination free and reconstruct any number of unlikely voyages. Interestingly enough, a similar phenomenon takes place for one weekend each autumn on a bald hilltop just north of the tiny Clay County burg of Rollag—but this fantasy is a collective one and it relates to a much more recent era of prairie life.

It is the Western Minnesota Steam Threshers Reunion; a gathering of well more than 50,000 people each year, all of whom share a consuming interest in the age of steam. This, too, was an era that conjures up a distinctive and romantic imagery: the ponderous metal engines, the billowing smoke and steam, the wide leather belts that stretched great distances between wooden pulleys, the sweat and heat of the boiler. If this kind of thing calls to you, get yourself to Rollag Labor Day weekend for what locals claim is the largest gathering of steam engine enthusiasts in the world.

There are steam engines at the reunion of every imaginable size and shape—machines that were designed to perform a great range of tasks. There are threshing machines, saw mills, a steam-powered merry-go-round, three "Trains to Nowhere" that meander about on short stretches of track and several huge engines with flywheels up to 17 feet in diameter. In addition to all the hardware, there are also craft demonstrations, plenty of traditional foods and, capping off each day, a fiddlers' jamboree.

The landscape of this region varies from the mixed forest and farmland of the lake-strewn area north of Alexandria to the dead-flat alluvial plain of the Red River Valley. Inspiration Peak, which at 1,750 feet above sea level is one of Minnesota's higher points, is a great spot to get an overview of Vikingland's lake district, which draws many people to the area just north of Alexandria each summer. This conical hilltop, found on Otter Tail County Road 38 about 10 miles east of Minnesota Highway 78, is part of the Leaf Hills. They were formed by a glacier of the last ice age as it deposited huge piles of debris (moraine) at its terminus—hence the geological name, terminal moraine. The picnic grounds and hiking trails that flank the peak offer a nice spot for a wayside rest. The view from the top is well worth the hike up.

As you drive west and north from here, the terrain becomes increasingly flat and agricultural fields stretch as far as the eye can see. Still, here and there amidst the endless rows of crops that occupy 99.5 percent of Minnesota's original prairies, there are occasional refuges set aside to

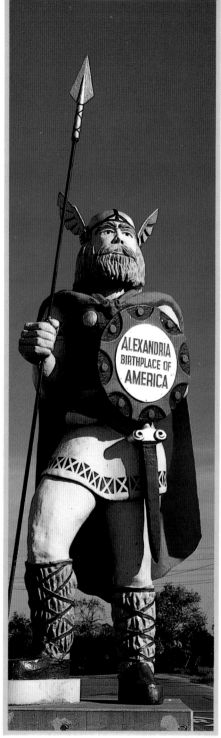

CONNIE WANNER PHOTOS

Left: Pride in their Norse heritage and a firm belief in the legitimacy of the Kensington runestone inspired Alexandria residents to erect this Viking statue downtown.
Below: Moorhead's Heritage Hjemkomst Interpretive center is the final home of the good ship Hjemkomst.

Facing page: Whether or not Vikings made their way to western Minnesota in the late 14th century, the possibility helped inspire the construction in the 1970s of the Viking ship Hjemkomst ("Homecoming") by Robert Asp, a Moorhead-area teacher. The ship completed an epic voyage from Duluth to Bergen, Norway in 1982.

Prairie chicken males leapt toward each other, collided in the air and landed to engage in a little self-righteous foot stomping.

allow the once-pervasive prairie grasses to regain a small foot-hold. And it is on these enclaves that each spring the interested visitor can witness one of the most striking rituals in Minnesota's animal kingdom: the courtship of the prairie chicken.

The areas of short-cropped grasses preferred by the prairie chicken for their amorous encounters are called booming grounds because of the distinctive sound made by the male of the species during the ritual. To observe this singular event in the Moorhead area, you should make prior arrangements with the Nature Conservancy in Glyndon or, if you're near Crookston, contact the Minnesota Prairie Chicken Society, which manages booming grounds in Polk County.

Determined to get to the booming grounds before the chickens did (and run the risk of scaring them off), I arrived at a squat Nature Conservancy canvas blind in the middle of a huge open field well before first light on a rainy and cold April morning. To stave off the chill I took along a Thermos of coffee. A camera with a telephoto lens and a notebook completed my armaments. Not long after I'd become accustomed to the drip of the rain through the seams and creases of the blind, the chickens began to stir. A most unusual display of aviary histrionics gradually unfolded before me.

First, while it was still too dark to see anything, came the booming. I could hear what later proved to be eight or nine chickens—it sounded like a small army—proceeding slowly across the ground until they surrounded my blind. In the growing light I began to be able to discern the males, each looking rather like a jowly rabbit, preparing for each round of whooping by raising special feathers on the backs of their necks into a vertical position. The uplifted feathers revealed bright orange air sacs which the chickens puffed into fullness and then deflated as they let out an unforgettable penetrating three-toned whoop.

Often the males did their booming while squared off in pairs, head to head. They leapt toward each other, collided in the air and landed to engage in a little self-righteous foot stomping accompanied by the appropriate sound effects. The birds gave off a variety of other noises too, resembling, among other things, tropical bird calls, cooing, cackling and the disturbingly realistic sound of an infant crying. They kept up this cacophony for several hours, during which the sun eventually came out, allowing for some fine photo opportunities.

Curious to find out exactly what all this activity was about, after the chickens suddenly flew off to some nearby trees, I visited the Nature Conservancy manager, Brian Winter, at his home in Glyndon. Brian explained that the general scenario I had witnessed had to do with each male defending his self-designated breeding territory (usually an area of ground roughly oval in shape) against other nearby males while simultaneously trying to attract the attentions of any females in the vicinity. The idea is that any male who is able to intimidate his fellows by putting on a better show expands the size of his breeding grounds, thereby increasing the chances of having a desirable hen stroll into his life.

CONNIE WANNER

Facing page: The prairie chicken, once a common creature on the short-grass prairies of western Minnesota, still can be observed practicing its fascinating courting ritual each spring. *Left:* A little "prairie-chicken" pride, shows along I-94 at Rothsay.

WESTERN MINNESOTA STEAM THRESHERS REUNION

Each Labor Day weekend, the tiny town of Rollag roars to life for the Western Minnesota Steam Threshers Reunion, an event that some claim is the largest gathering of steam-engine enthusiasts in the world (that's what they'll tell you at the Rollag Store, anyway). The celebration includes an example of just about every artifact ever made that ran on steam— including tractors, threshers, trains, merry-go-rounds, sawmills and several monstrous engines.

62

Itasca State Park
Sawmill Creek
Forest
History Center
Hafeman
Boat Works

Above and facing page: Lake Itasca holds an irresistible fascination. Endowed with near-mythical qualities as the long-sought source of North America's greatest river, it is also the centerpiece of Minnesota's first and grandest state park. Here you can find the state's tallest red and white pines, a prehistoric bison-kill site and acres of stately, towering trees with the solemnity of a cathedral.

HEADWATERS TERRITORY

One of the most intriguing aspects of the white man's relationship with the Mississippi River is that it took such a remarkably long time for anyone to find its source. Nearly three centuries had passed since the Mississippi had first been seen by a European, Hernando de Soto, in 1541, and still the river's origins remained a mystery. Meanwhile, other much more arduous feats of exploration already had been accomplished by the new masters of the New World. Both Alexander MacKenzie in 1793 and the Lewis and Clark expedition in 1804-1806 had charted vast terrains while seeking the mythical Northwest Passage. But cartographers still were forced to draw maps of the United States that left in question the source of the mightiest river in the land.

The white man's first attempt to follow the Father of Waters to its northernmost reaches was lead by a 26-year-old U.S. Army officer, Zebulon Montgomery Pike. In the wake of the Louisiana Purchase, he was sent upriver in 1805 to establish sites for frontier American military outposts, to attempt to make peace between the warring Ojibway and Dakota, to gather information on British traders occupying American soil and, if all that weren't enough, to find the source of the Mississippi. His journey took him as far north as what is now called Cass Lake, which he erroneously took to be the river's source.

The next white explorer, Michigan Territorial Governor Lewis Cass, duplicated Pike's journey in 1820. His expedition included a geologist named Henry Rowe Schoolcraft, who officially concurred with his leader's assertion that Cass Lake was indeed the Mississippi's point of origin, although Schoolcraft evidently had private thoughts to the contrary. For, in 1832, as U.S. Government agent to the Ojibway Indians at the Lake Superior settlement of Sault Ste. Marie,

Schoolcraft returned to the Mississippi. In the dozen years since his last visit to the area a flamboyant Italian adventurer, Giacomo Constantino Beltrami, had made the dubious claim that he had found a lake, which he called Lake Julia, that was both the source of the Mississippi and the Red River of the North. Schoolcraft's intentions were to lay this matter finally to rest.

Assisted by his wife, a woman of Ojibway and British descent, Schoolcraft learned the Ojibway language and tribal customs. Through his contacts with the Ojibway, he employed a well qualified guide, Yellow Head, who led him from Cass Lake upstream to a small lake that the Ojibway called Elk Lake. Upon his arrival, Schoolcraft hung his hat on a tree and officially proclaimed that Elk Lake was henceforth to be called Lake Itasca—a name that he created by some clever blending of syllables from the Latin, *ver*ITAS CA*put*, "true head."

This great geographical landmark has been preserved for future generations as Itasca State Park, Minnesota's first—and in many ways grandest—state park. In fact, the place feels a little like a miniature Yellowstone or Yosemite. Itasca's preponderant historic significance infuses the woods with a sense of solemnity. The park's meandering roadways seem to encourage drivers to prowl along at an admiring pace. The trees are gracious and stately, and include in their number Minnesota's largest white and red pines on record. Also, the use of huge white pine logs in the construction of the park's buildings reinforces the larger-than-life quality.

Itasca is the only state park in Minnesota that has a lodge offering meals and accommodations. It is also the only place along the Mississippi's 2,348-mile course to the sea where the river can be crossed as readily as if you were hopping from stone to stone on a garden path. Lake Itasca is clean and

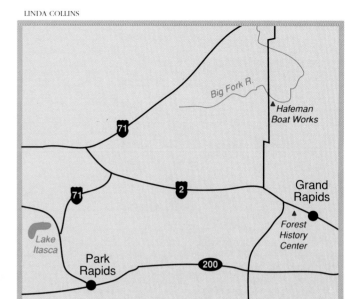

Two sites bring the logging boom vividly back to life.

sparkling, and the water that begins its epic southern journey by flowing northward at a mere trickle is all but transparent—here the river's popular nickname, Big Muddy, is laughingly out of place.

The logging boom that swept through northern Minnesota's extensive pine forests around the turn of the century can be explored in detail at two sites in the vicinity of Itasca State Park. Sawmill Creek, a reconstructed logging town just east of Park Rapids, is clearly oriented to profit from the tourist dollar, but it has some interesting features that make the place worthy of a visit. Foremost among these are a working steam-powered sawmill, planer mill and shingle mill that employees use to produce lumber for a related log-building construction business. There are some three dozen log and wood-frame structures that make up Sawmill Creek's various historic (and some not-so-historic) businesses, including a newspaper, smithy and various craft industries.

The best learning opportunity related to Minnesota's logging history, however, is found just west of Grand Rapids on Itasca County Road 70 at the Minnesota Historical Society-run Forest History Center. The center combines a modern interpretive center with an exactingly recreated logging camp, circa 1900. Exhibits on the history of the relationships that Minnesotans—both Native American and of European descent—have maintained with their forests are the focus of the

 Logging's importance as an historic and contemporary industry is amply evident in and around Itasca State Park. Grand white pine logs form part of Itasca's buildings *(facing page, top)*. In Grand Rapids, where today's economy relies on timber harvest and paper production, the Forest History Center provides information on forest ecology, as in the fire display *(facing page, bottom)*. Other exhibits at the interpretive center prepare visitors for the rough-hewn lifestyle of lumber camp cooks *(this page, far left)*, lumberjacks *(below)* and blacksmiths *(left)* at the center's reconstructed logging camp.

*Besides providing pine for saw timber and hardwood species for paper production, the boreal forests of northern Minnesota, which are thick with aspen and birch **(right)**, have supported an ancient industry that barely survives into the 20th century. Master bark canoe builder Ray Boessel **(facing page)** continues the tradition set by his grandfather-in-law, Bill Hafeman, at his shop on the banks of the Big Fork River north of Grand Rapids.*

BETH C. SUNDIN

displays at the interpretive center. The rough-hewn and bawdy lifestyles of the men and women (there were a few) who made a living bringing down the big pine are brought to life in the Northwoods Logging Company camp, located a short walk through the woods.

The period characters occupying the camp and a nearby 1930s Forest Service ranger cabin—from the crude stable boss to the ornery cook and her timid assistants to the solitary saw sharpener—play their well researched roles with robust spirits. They have no reservations about asking you to share the work load either. When I was there, a concerted attempt was made to enlist a couple of visitors in signing on to assist in the kitchen or to fill the bottom-rung position of "road monkey." We learned that the latter ignoble task, which probably was the only thing any of us were actually qualified for, entailed throwing straw down in front of the heavy log-burdened sleighs (logging was a winter pursuit) to slow them on the icy downhills. Better yet, road monkeys also collected "road apples" left in the wake of the big draft horses. No one signed up, but we all had a good laugh considering who among us would be best suited for the job.

One of Minnesota's premier woodland industries that for centuries epitomized the blending of aesthetic tastes and functional needs was the crafting of the birchbark canoe. A well made bark canoe is light to carry, paddles efficiently, is surprisingly resilient and is a pleasure to behold. Once the workhorse of the lake-strewn forests, the birchbark canoe now is built by only a handful of builders. And, appropriately enough, one of the best of this dying breed welcomes visitors to his humble canoe shop along the banks of the Big Fork River, about 50 miles north of Grand Rapids on Minnesota Highway 6.

Ray Boessel inherited his one-man operation from his grandfather-in-law, Bill Hafeman, whose name still reigns on a sign above the door of the tar-paper shop. Bill taught himself to make canoes in the 1920s out of necessity. At that time the paddle to town offered greater chances of arriving safely than did travel on the area's rudimentary roads. Ray explains that Bill's first canoe effort got him into town quickly enough—it took just four hours—but the craft deteriorated so badly in the process that the return trip took two days. Inspection of one of the lovely canoes on display in and around the shop is ample proof that Bill and his successor have come a long way since that first effort.

In his gentle manner, Ray is happy to explain just how he goes about the painstaking process of making a canoe from scratch. In early summer he harvests his own bark from paper birch trees (lacking in stature, he notes, as compared to those of former times). He also visits spruce swamps to secure long sections of spruce root—the preferred material for lashing together the sections of bark skin and the structural supports, which are commonly made of white cedar. Then, once all materials are prepared for construction, he assembles the bark skin first and inserts an interlocking network of planking, steam-bent ribs, gunwales and thwarts.

Conditions permitting, visitors are welcome to take one of his masterpieces on a test paddle. I did so and was surprised to find the canoe so easily responsive to my touch. It also took an indignant bump against a rounded boulder without complaint. Above all, I loved the way the canoe gently creaked like a large basket under my weight. If you're tempted, as I was, to take one of these beauties home with you, be prepared for the four-digit price tag.

JOHN G. SHEPARD

Soudan Mine
Hill Annex Mine
Ironworld
Hibbing

The 1924-vintage hoist at the quarter-mile–deep Tower Soudan underground mine (above) and the gaping water-filled pit at the Hill Annex Mine (facing page) are tangible reminders of the once-mighty iron ore industry of northern Minnesota. Both these intriguing state parks offer visitors opportunities to explore mining history, evolving technology and the lifestyles of the Iron Range's ethnically diverse population.

THE IRON TRAIL

First came the bonanza of the fur trade. Then logging. And by the time the mineral rush hit northern Minnesota at the end of the 19th century, there was a certain pattern to the way that these enterprises worked themselves out on the land. The pattern was established in the days of the fur trade, and it revolved around two facts. Number one was that the European hunger for fur was monstrous. Second, the men who came to Minnesota to establish their fortunes feeding this insatiable giant lacked restraint.

The early traders encountered boreal forests that spread northward seemingly to infinity. The forests were thick with fur-bearing creatures that the Indians were willing to trap and barter for European manufactured goods. And with no checks built into the system and no particular concern for the environment exhibited by the traders, the beaver nearly met the same fate as did the bison of the Great Plains.

Then came the clear-cut logging boom and with it the virtual disappearance of the forests themselves—forests that had been thick with stately red and white pine. Today, except in the Boundary Waters Canoe Area wilderness, where about half the land never has been logged, virgin reds and whites are found only in occasional solitary stands. And with these big pines went the inland caribou, displaced by white-tail deer who thrived on the poplar and birch that sprang up where the pines fell.

As one might expect, iron mining in Minnesota has followed a similar path. And it is a path that can be traced by visiting a number of historic sites that run down the backbone and flank the edges of one of the world's greatest iron ranges: the Mesabi.

Mesabi was a name given by the Ojibway to a mythological giant whose lair was beneath a wooded range of hills northwest of Duluth. Having once roamed about the region, the giant was thought by the Indians to be finally at rest, and so he was...until he awoke with a tremendous roar in the late 1860s at the prodding of the white man.

Minnesota's first iron mine was established not far from Lake Vermilion by a couple of local entrepreneurs backed by Eastern mining capitalist Charlemain Tower. Their attention was first drawn to the Lake Vermilion area by rumors of a gold rush that turned out to be a bust. But where there wasn't gold there was iron ore—in quantities and of such quality that the Tower Soudan underground mine, which proved to be the richest iron mine in the state, yielded chunks of ore so pure that in their raw state they could be welded together.

The Soudan mine, just east of Tower on Route 169, has been preserved by the Minnesota Department of Natural Resources as one of Minnesota's most fascinating historic sites. The tour involves a three-minute ride in a rattling elevator down to the mine's lowest level, 2,341 feet below the surface. Here a small train takes visitors a quarter of a mile down a horizontal tunnel, or "drift," to arrive at a recreated work site. Mannequins are posed ready to operate deafening carbide-tipped air-powered drills, their work illuminated only by the headlamps they wore.

Still, you learn from your guide, these conditions were a great improvement over the early days when miners labored for 12-hour shifts, wielding picks and shovels by the light of candles. The train that transported the ore back to the central shaft was preceded by teams of mules that stayed below ground for six-month shifts. When brought up to the surface for six months of well deserved vacation, to prevent blindness, the mules had their eyes wrapped in gauze, which was removed slowly over the course of a week.

As the iron ore industry grew in Minnesota, the hard hematite ore that the Soudan mine yielded, and the under-

ground mining it required, proved to be the exception rather than the rule for Minnesota's iron resources. Most ore on the Mesabi Range (the Soudan mine was on the adjacent Vermilion range) was of a rare powdery consistency that baffled early prospectors. It quickly became apparent that the most efficient way to gather this ore was to use the strip mining techniques that have altered the appearance of the landscape dramatically.

At the western end of the Mesabi, at the town of Calumet, the Department of Natural Resources has preserved one of these open pit mines as Minnesota's 64th and newest state park. After a visit to the interpretive center at the Hill Annex Mine, where exhibits illuminate the changing technologies and lifestyles of the miners who labored here from 1903 until 1978, prepare for a one-and-one-half-hour bus tour of the gaping pit itself.

The Hill Annex wasn't particularly huge by Mesabi standards, but this fact somehow serves to make the place seem even more gigantic. From the top of slag piles hundreds of feet above the now-flooded floor of the mine, as my bus rumbled along the dusty roads, I felt as if I were traveling through a fantastic moonscape occupied here and there by giant rusting steam shovels, which, in their abandoned state, gave the place the feeling of an archaeological site in process of excavation.

When the iron rush hit, northern Minnesota became a favored destination for laborers hailing from all over Europe. These immigrants brought with them a fabulous wealth of cultural traditions that have been chronicled in a wide range of stimulating hands-on displays at Ironworld, the Iron Range's $8.5 million interpretive center and entertainment complex, which you'll find on Route 169 at Chisholm.

Ironworld's first-rate living history exhibits are concerned primarily with the human side of iron ore mining on the range. Traditional foods and crafts from Italy to Eastern Europe are well represented and available for purchase. There are exhibits on family life, too, and on subjects like the rise of the labor movement and the role that mining played during two world wars. Regular concerts are held in an outdoor garden area and in an acoustically acclaimed outdoor amphitheater. And train and trolley rides are available along the rims of several spectacular nearby open pit mines.

The Soudan mine **(below)**—*Minnesota's oldest, deepest and richest iron mine—was a model operation that took the lives of only 13 miners during 60 years of operation. Tours led by former miners impart a vivid sense of what working 2,341 feet below ground was like. Conditions at open pit mines like the Hill Annex* **(facing page)** *were quite different. Seventy-five years of blasting and hauling created enormous canyons and towering hills of discarded materials separated from iron ore by on-site processing plants.*

KENT & DONNA DANNEN

LINDA COLLINS

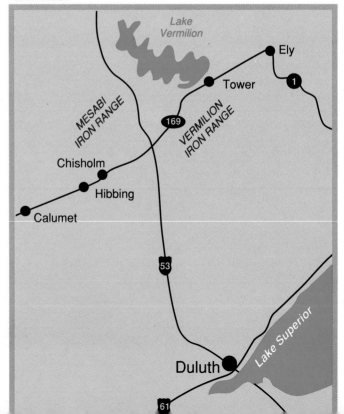

Hibbing High School, built during the boom time of the early 1920s, cost nearly $4 million, paid for by U.S. Steel.

As fascinating and well presented as all this is, however, it was while touring Hibbing's palatial high school that I felt I most fully appreciated the spirit of the miners whose labors were so crucial to the creation of America's industrial might. The school, I learned from my tour guide, was built in the boom time of the early 1920s at a cost of nearly $4 million. It was paid for almost entirely by U.S. Steel as a gesture to the population, which was forced to pick up and move to accommodate the hungry maw of an expanding open pit mine. The story goes that the immigrant miners highly valued education as a way for their children to realize the promise of their new land. The spectacular school building is both a testament to that fact and an expression of the bosses' paternalistic generosity.

I was transfixed by a long rectangular mural on the school's library wall, circa 1913, by David T. Workman, that celebrates the epic conversion of Mesabi iron ore into steel. Workers representing 16 of the Iron Range's 34 prominent immigrant groups are shown united in earnest labor made hallowed by an aura of golden light. At one end of this panorama, at the edge of northern Minnesota's now largely deci-

mated wilderness, there stands an attentive deer beside the gnarled trunks of grand, sun-dappled white pine. At the other end there is the heavy but somehow safe and wholesome industrial darkness of the steel mills where anonymous workers are dwarfed by a huge cauldron spilling liquid sun. In between, the miners strain with picks and shovels and work the levers of primitive cranes. Ore boats accept their burden at the docks of a pristine Lake Superior beneath fair skies. A quotation borders the painting at either end: "They force the blunt and yet unblooded steel to do their will," by Cooper, and, "Lifting the hidden iron that glimpses in laboured mines undrainable of ore," from Tennyson.

The students sprinkled about the library were working quietly and with apparent industry. Everywhere in the building there was order and cleanliness. Hallways illuminated by recessed lights to show off the hand-sculpted plaster mouldings and arched ceilings were completely free from litter. Open classroom doors revealed more students listening respectfully to their teachers. And in the school's resplendent auditorium, which is watched over by several sensuous plaster-of-paris muses and crowned by two large Czech crystal chandeliers (made in Belgium in 1920 for $15,000 apiece), the varnished wooden backs of row after row of gold crushed-velvet-upholstered seats were completely devoid of marks made by the idle whittler or graffiti artist.

How could students not be swayed by such a setting, I thought to myself as I set out for the observation platform of the Hull Rust Mahoning mine. Their school is possessed by the labors and aspirations of their parents and grandparents and the expectation of a better life afforded through education adorns the very walls. Surely, the students I had seen were on their way to big things and high places.

Then I entered what remains of the old Hibbing—a grid of streets bordered by weedy sidewalks and an occasional wrought iron street lamp. Where front porches once ran block after block there are now a series of plaques explaining who lived in the modest homes that occupied the many vacant lots, each knee-high in grasses.

A little farther along I arrived at the observation deck of the Hull Rust Mahoning mine—the largest open pit iron mine in the world and the place to go if you want to see what has become of the rest of the old Hibbing. A chain-link fence in front of the interpretive center lined the top of a cliff that drops 535 feet to the bottom of the now-flooded mine. A mile away on the far shore was a raw and red terraced hillside where massive cranes with house-sized shovels were at work scooping up chunks of ore that had been blasted free of the earth's grip. The cranes dropped their loads with a silent cloud of dust into 170-ton dump trucks, each with a tiny driver's compartment high above the giant front left wheel. When loaded, these trucks crawled like mechanical snails toward some unseen processing plant beyond the top of a distant ridge.

Through operations like this one, the top grade ore on the Mesabi Range was exhausted by the early 1960s. Improvements in technology then made the mining of lower grade taconite a feasible undertaking and the mines continued to thrive until economic conditions of the late 1970s brought about another, more profound slump in the industry. Now only a few mines like the Hull Rust Mahoning have been able to maintain their operations as the remaining traces of the Ojibway's now largely depleted Mesabi—the once-sleeping giant—are being scooped up and hauled away.

LEE BLOOMQUIST PHOTOS BOTH PAGES

*Mining life continues at Hibbing, where the Hull Rust Mahoning mine **(left)**, the world's largest open pit iron mine, still operates. The value that immigrant miners placed on education is evident at the grand Hibbing High School. A library mural **(below)** captures the epic proportions of the mining process.*

Facing page: *Ironworld USA was built in 1985 as a major interpretive and entertainment center for visitors to Minnesota's Iron Range. The $8.5 million complex celebrates ethnic diversity and traditions of area miners through excellent craft, culinary and history exhibits.*

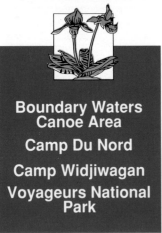

**Boundary Waters
Canoe Area**

Camp Du Nord

Camp Widjiwagan

**Voyageurs National
Park**

*Above and facing page: The song
of the common loon, Minnesota's
state bird, is at once eerie, lonely
and welcoming. The lakes of canoe
country are prime locations for
seeing this beautiful bird—and
for catching trophy walleye,
northern pike, lake trout and bass.*

BORDER ROUTE TREK

The first thing you notice as you pile out of your canoe-laden car at the shore of Fall Lake at the edge of the Boundary Waters Canoe Area (BWCA) is that something is missing. The mechanized tedium of cruising hour after hour at speeds unknown to humankind until a little more than a century ago has abruptly ceased. The last echoes of the tape player and the slamming of car doors are absorbed into the surrounding forest. Suddenly, it's very quiet.

An imperceptible breeze seems to move about the lake, kicking up the surface into an intricate pattern of ripples that dance in the golden sunlight.

Overhead a couple of towering white pines are standing immobile with unfathomable patience and dignity—a discipline they have maintained for the last 250 years.

Across the bay a loon calls into the approaching dusk. Her message is filled at once with welcome and with longing and with something unrecognizable—something beyond what we know.

Your first paddle strokes send tiny whirlpools drifting sternward to propel you into a water-scape and landscape that, for all appearances, has changed little since the days when the canoe was Minnesota's primary means of travel. You're only five minutes away from the asphalt ribbon that leads back into the late 20th century, and already you suspect the truth: there's no better antidote to civilization as we know it than a paddle-powered excursion into the BWCA.

The Boundary Waters' million-plus acres of clear waterways and thick boreal forests qualify as the largest wilderness area east of the Mississippi River. It is literally America's canoeing mecca, drawing tens of thousands of adventurers each year from all over the country and abroad in search of experiences of a wholly different order than those that civilization can provide.

Back-country canoe travel requires each person to carry all of his or her belongings within the confines of a couple of packs that fit neatly between the gunwales of a craft that has changed little in the last 1,500 years. The material world, by this measure, is suddenly reduced to delightfully simple proportions.

There is great satisfaction in meeting the challenges of the wilderness and indulging in its many pleasures—a joy distinguished by the fact that the satisfaction is unmistakably of one's own creation. Fresh trout cooked over the open fire tastes doubly delicious when you know that you were cunning enough to fill the larder. An afternoon swimming in cool waters and sunning on the Boundary Water's ancient pre-Cambrian bedrock is all the more welcome on the heels of a morning spent paddling into a head wind. Canoeists who choose to undergo a difficult portage often find that the effort required to haul their gear through the woods from lake to lake is more than compensated for by the satisfaction of arriving under one's own power at a pristine goal.

Newcomers to the Boundary Waters can arrange for fully outfitted and, in some cases, guided trips by contacting the many outfitters located at jumping-off points like Ely, the Gunflint Trail or Grand Marais. To control the flow of people through this ecologically sensitive area, the U.S. Forest Service manages a permit system. Reservations for permits should be sought far in advance, especially during such peak travel times as holidays and weekends.

Before heading into the wilds, all travelers should become familiar with appropriate camping and travel etiquette for canoe country—both to ensure a safe trip and to protect the lakes and forests for generations to come. Outfitters can provide some pre-trip orientation, though groups with little canoe tripping experience should find a

At one point or another in canoe country, almost everyone finds himself indulging in the thought of being deliciously alone.

qualified leader or a guide who is knowledgeable in wilderness navigation, canoeing, camping and first aid skills.

A Boundary Waters canoe trip can be planned to suit a variety of interests. Anglers can consult with outfitters to locate the best waters for catching lake trout, bass, walleye and northern pike. Those looking for a physical challenge can plan trips that cover new ground each day on circular routes that connect a series of lakes so that the starting point is also the finish. A number of rivers wind through the Boundary Waters, too, providing a change of pace from lake paddling. And, an alternative for those seeking a leisurely get-away is to find a prime campsite an easy day's paddle from the trail head and set up a base camp from which areas close at hand can be explored without having to haul all the gear along.

Regardless of the nature of the trip, at one point or another almost everyone in canoe country finds himself indulging in the thought that one is finally, deliciously alone. Often this occurs on an isolated lake a portage or two off the beaten path, where civilization seems to be centuries away and, surrounding on all sides, is only nature's glory.

However, the facts, as archaeologists have been slowly discovering since the late 1970s, speak to the contrary. Although the Boundary Waters appear to be pristine and truly wild, physical evidence of human activity in the area dating back to the end of the last Ice Age abounds.

The first inhabitants of the region were among the earliest human occupants of North America and the first predecessors of today's Native Americans. The Paleo ("old") Indians, as they are now called, arrived about 10,000 years ago as the last wave of glaciers receded to the north. These nomadic hunters survived on caribou, moose and now-extinct forms of bison in a tundra-like environment that resembled today's Barren Grounds far to the north. A few exquisitely crafted spear points three to six inches in length, made of locally quarried stone, comprise the only tangible evidence of these hunters' existence. Interestingly, these stone tools, presumed to have been made according to a ritualized manufacturing process, represent the height of craftsmanship throughout the prehistoric record.

Scientists believe that the dugout canoe made its first appearance in what is now the BWCA during the Archaic period, which began about 7,000 years ago. This was a period of warmer and drier climate than that found today. It also was the first time since the Ice Age that the woods were thick with the same three pine species prevalent now.

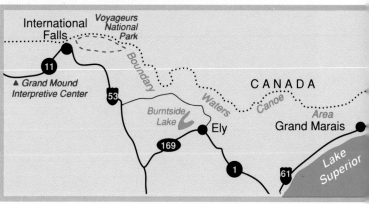

DANIEL J. COX

Left: *Canoe routes through the Boundary Waters Canoe Area have been traveled for centuries by trappers, fur traders and legendary French-Canadian voyageurs. The area's original inhabitants—nomadic native hunters and gatherers whose ancestors migrated from Asia—have left signs of their passing in the form of pictographs, or rock paintings, made with natural dies* **(facing page).**

Evidence has been found of large stone and copper wood-working tools that appear to have been well suited for carving canoes.

By the end of the Archaic period, about 200 B.C., the climate had cooled to its current range of temperatures. Birch and aspen trees appeared in greater numbers, and at some point the material of choice for building canoes became bark. Other cultural changes that occurred during this time include the disappearance of copper as a manufacturing material, the first use of pottery and the construction of large burial mounds. Some of these mounds can be seen today west of the BWCA at Grand Mound Interpretive Center (located on Minnesota Highway 11, 17 miles west of International Falls).

It was at the end of this prehistoric era, in the 1700s, that the first European explorers, missionaries and fur traders penetrated into canoe country. The French-Canadian voyageurs who traveled the lakes and rivers in large birch bark freight canoes weighted with tons of beaver pelts have left evidence of their passing at occasional campsites and abandoned trading posts. Also, numerous artifacts discovered underwater at the base of several rapids along the international border—a heavily traveled route through the ages—indicate that the challenges of the wilderness occasionally got the better of these hardy adventurers.

Prehistoric paddlers and the first Europeans had much the same tastes in campsites as do today's recreational canoeists. Sites that have been most heavily used over the centuries tend to be on exposed, elevated points with good visibility and some exposure to the prevailing breezes. Unfortunately, many of these sites have been so heavily used and subjected to such erosion that any evidence of prehistoric lifestyles has been washed away.

Although arrowheads, pieces of scrap flint and pottery shards have been found on about 35 percent of all BWCA campsites, canoeists should keep in mind that it is illegal to

*In every season, the Canadian border country offers special gifts to wilderness travelers. Hardy winter adventurers traverse lakes and portage routes by ski, snowshoe, dog sled and snowmobile **(below)**. Autumn is a great time for hiking, hunting and late-season fishing **(facing page)**.*

DANIEL J. COX

81

disturb any artifacts encountered during their travels. The record of human life in canoe country is a delicate one that easily can be destroyed, and many questions about it have yet to be answered.

Through the coordinated efforts of the U.S. Forest Service, the St. Paul YMCA, the North Star Ski Club and some resort owners who have glimpsed the tremendous possibilities that the region holds, the BWCA in the Ely area has become an increasingly popular winter destination for skiers demanding well designed, maintained trails as an alternative to the miles of untracked wilderness.

The largest network of established trails near Ely is clustered mostly inside the BWCA on the north arm of Burntside Lake, about 17 miles northwest of town. Intermediate and advanced loops and several easier trails wander for more than 80 kilometers through woods that are home not only to the elusive eastern timber wolf but also to moose, deer and a wealth of small game.

*Summer attracts water sports enthusiasts from all over North America and beyond. Travel in the Boundary Water Canoe Area wilderness is restricted to canoe and kayak **(below right)**. Cabins on the edge of the Boundary Waters can provide opportunities for day trips into the wilderness **(below left)**. Voyageurs National Park, near International Falls, is a perfect setting for motor-powered excursions **(facing page).***

R. HAMILTON SMITH PHOTOS

82

Stands of huge virgin white pine with names like the Sentinels and the Old Druid Pines complement several striking ridgetop vistas. Lake crossings offer easy skiing for beginners and opportunities for ski skaters. Because motorized vehicles are prohibited in the BWCA, these trails are not groomed and tracked; however, they are well maintained, well marked and used often enough that visiting skiers usually need not be concerned with having to break trail.

Fifteen miles northeast of Ely near Jasper Lake is another network of trails, this one groomed both for diagonal striders (30 kilometers) and skaters (15 kilometers). The Jasper Hills trail system lies on gentler terrain than that found along the north arm of Burntside Lake. Skiers are surrounded on three sides by the BWCA and the Canadian border is only a four-mile back-country trek to the north. The pre-Cambrian bedrock has been molded into rolling ridges over which trails meander through stands of pine, cedar, aspen and birch. Jasper and Tofte lakes offer flat-track skiing for novices on a trail that follows the base of an impressive lichen-covered cliff.

If skiing through pristine woodlands on a well marked trail is a little too tame for your tastes, there are outfitters and outdoor education centers in the Ely area that can provide more intimate and challenging encounters with the surrounding wilds. For families and groups, St. Paul YMCA camps Du Nord and Widjiwagan near the North Arm trail system provide structured interpretive activities with trained naturalists as well as inexpensive accommodations. The Voyageur Outward Bound School on the banks of the Kawishiwi River leads small groups of students into the woods on challenging ski and dog sled journeys that are designed to enhance personal growth and effectiveness. Polar explorer Paul Schurke's Wintergreen Treks on White Iron Lake also offers guided back-country skiing and dog sledding trips.

While the Boundary Waters wilderness has been set

On land or on water, Boundary Waters offers year-round recreation opportunities.

DANIEL J. COX

83

aside specifically for those who prefer a non-motorized escape into the back country, 219,000-acre Voyageurs National Park is another pristine enclave along the Minnesota-Ontario border that welcomes power boaters and snowmobilers as well as canoeists and skiers. Voyageurs, Minnesota's only national park, is accessible east of International Falls from Highway 11 or from the south along Highway 53. All roads end at the park's boundaries. It is one of the few national parks that must be explored by some means of travel other than the automobile.

Excursion boats run by a National Park Service concessionaire depart the Rainy Lake Visitors Center on Black Bay and Kabetogama Lake Visitors Center nearly every day. Many trips feature interpretive naturalists who explain the park's interesting natural and cultural history as you cruise its open waters. Houseboats can be rented from several outfitters in the area, and the many resorts along Koochiching County Road 11 east of International Falls, at Kabetogama Lake, Ash River and Crane Lake can supply you with everything you need for a deluxe fishing excursion into the back country.

The Kettle Falls Hotel, arguably Minnesota's most remote and historically intriguing hotel, is located deep in Voyageurs National Park on the Kabetogama Peninsula. Reached only by boat, this tastefully renovated establishment first catered to loggers who spent their winters deep in the fast-disappearing pine forests during the early decades of this century. In keeping with their rough-hewn tastes, the Kettle Falls gained an early reputation as a back-country bordello and saloon, although the hotel register indicates that people of some refinement—including logging company owners and their associates—also frequented the place. In any event, you'll more than likely find today's guests and the hotel's relaxed hospitality amiable enough.

For toll-free information on border country recreation and lodging call: the Ely Chamber of Commerce at 800-422-9653, ext. 48; the Gunflint Trail Association at 800-328-3362, or the Tip of the Arrowhead Association at 800-622-4014.

For BWCA permit reservations write: Reservations, Superior National Forest, Box 338, Duluth 55801 or call: 218-720-5440.

For information on Voyageurs National Park, call 218-283-9821. For lodging information, call the International Falls Chamber of Commerce (218-283-9400) or the International Falls Travel Information Center (218-285-7623).

*In the remote reaches of Voyageurs National Park, an environment perhaps best described as a water-scape **(facing page),** is Minnesota's most remote and historically colorful hotel. The Kettle Falls Hotel **(left)** has been restored to its former glory as a turn-of-the-century outpost serving the varied appetites of northwoods loggers who spent winters cutting giant red and white pines. Houseboats **(below)** provide another form of accommodation for modern-day visitors.*

Cascade River

**North Shore
Ski Trails**

**Jay Cooke
State Park**

St. Louis River

Duluth

*There are no tides and the off-shore breezes don't smell of salt, but in almost all other respects the cold, clear waters of Lake Superior may as well be an ocean. The rugged Minnesota shoreline with cliffs like the looming Palisade Head (**facing page**), was built to the same larger-than-life scale.*

THE NORTH SHORE

The spectacle of Ted Young bringing order to his clamoring Alaskan husky sled-dog team is like an arctic version of the Keystone Kops.

Grabbing the front of the nylon harness with both hands and planting his heavy felt-lined boots into the snow, he drags his two big lead dogs, Rose and Penny, around 180 degrees so that they are facing the brilliant white expanse of Poplar Lake. Then—commanding, coaxing, pleading—he turns his attention to untangling the rest of the throng.

Meanwhile, Rose and Penny circle around behind him to see what the continued ruckus is about. All is chaos and crossed lines once again, the hapless musher stuck in the middle.

"The problem," Young says as the dogs finally fall silent and begin eagerly pulling our sled toward the distant pine-studded shoreline, "is the heat. The dogs function best between zero and 30 below."

The trail over the deep snow pack has been warmed above freezing by southerly March breezes and a glorious, penetrating sun. And although the dogs apparently are a little dopey from the balmy weather, I sit comfortably on the sled's wooden frame, face tilted sunward, quite content with conditions just as they are.

I joined Ted Young and his dog team midway through a four-day exploration of one of North America's best kept winter secrets: Minnesota's Lake Superior shore and the woodlands surrounding the rugged Gunflint Trail.

Many canoeists and anglers are familiar with the vast region of clear lakes and virgin pine forests that make up the northeastern corner of the North Star State. The Boundary Waters Canoe Area annually attracts thousands of outdoor enthusiasts from all over the country to paddle or hike through a glacier-carved landscape that is home to delicious walleye and lake trout as well as timber wolves, moose and eagles.

However, as far as the skiing public is concerned, Minnesota's Arrowhead is still by and large *terra incognita*. The 70 to 100 inches of snow that annually cover this pristine terrain supports hundreds of miles of well maintained cross-country ski trails served by hospitable lodges. There are a couple of alpine skiing resorts, too, and a few hearty outfitters such as Ted Young.

The most extensively developed part of the Arrowhead for skiers is a stretch of Lake Superior's dramatic shoreline northeast of Duluth, known as the North Shore. My journey began here at an attractive 50-year-old edifice of wood and stone called the Cascade Lodge, which sits nine miles southwest of the old logging and fishing town of Grand Marais.

The lodge is in the heart of the 129-mile groomed-and-tracked North Shore Mountains Ski Trail, a cross-country network with challenges for skiers of all skill levels. Nearby are more than a dozen resorts offering a variety of accommodations, from rustic cabins to modern condominiums to stately old-world style lodges.

Rising just after dawn, I slipped quietly out of my cozy log cabin for a solitary pre-breakfast ski in the three inches of light powder that had fallen the night before. My route took me toward the aptly named Cascade River along a moderately difficult trail that wound through stands of tall cedar and pine hung heavy with sparkling clumps of snow.

I paused for a moment in the morning's stillness on a bridge spanning the Cascade's steep gorge. The faint gurgling of the rapids rising through several openings in the ice far below was the only sound to be heard. Under way once again, I rounded a bend in the trail to find a pair of deer—

a buck and a doe—browsing in my path. For a long moment we stood frozen in place, their eyes fast upon me, before they bounded gracefully out of sight.

After breakfast I skied high atop a ridge behind the lodge where an overlook offered a grand view of Superior's oceanlike sweep to the south. Shades of cool blue and silver were reflected in the hazy sunlight. To the west were the slopes of Lutsen Mountain ski area, a downhill resort with 27 runs as much as a mile in length on four adjacent mountainsides. Also hidden among the thick carpet of trees along the shoreline were 11 other lodges and inns that cooperate with Cascade Lodge in offering a midweek lodge-to-lodge ski-through service. This arrangement allows guests to ski the North Shore trails for as many as five days while sampling a different lodge each night. Innkeepers shuttle gear to each day's destination in advance.

A second network of lodges that offer a somewhat different version of the ski-through experience can be found by turning inland at Grand Marais and driving for a half hour into the heart of the wilderness on a winding road whose name harks back to the area's early fur-trade history: The Gunflint Trail.

Two lodges at either end of a 96-mile ski trail system that roughly parallels the road provide skiers with such accoutrements as hot tubs, lantern-lighted trails for night skiing and delicious home-cooked meals served family style before a crackling fire. But in the dense forest that separates these civilized outposts from one another there is an exotic alternative for the adventuresome skier: three Mongolian yurts—canvas-covered, cylindrical, peaked-roof tents that are heated by woodstoves and staffed by Ted Young and his Boundary Country Trekking staff.

It was toward one of these yurts that Young and I were bounding in our six-dog-power sled the following day. After

Below: A whitetail doe is interrupted from browsing at the edge of a North Shore meadow. The elusive eastern timber wolf, which hunts deer, is another resident of the Minnesota Arrowhead country.

Facing page: High Falls on the Baptism River is Minnesota's second-highest waterfall—and among the most spectacular. Hikers reach this scenic spot via trails within Tettegouche State Park.

DANIEL J. COX

LINDA COLLINS

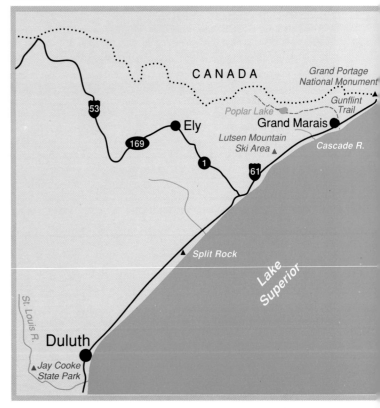

The North Shore Mountains ski trail offers a 129-mile groomed ski track among cabins and condominiums.

a brief stint with me at the helm of the sled and then a leisurely afternoon's ski on a gentle trail that was fresh with moose tracks, I arrived at Young's E.J. Croft hut in time for a much-touted Mongolian firepot dinner.

E.J. Croft, I learned from a plaque on the wall of the yurt that bore his name, was just the kind of person I'd always wanted to believe inhabited the northern forests. He was a "great pianist," the plaque said, who, between jobs shoveling snow for logging companies and putting in time as a commercial fisherman, claimed to have played 368 different pianos in his lifetime. He played with leather mittens on his hands and when that became dull he threw a blanket over the keys.

When it was finally presented in all its splendor, the Mongolian firepot dinner was received with the kind of enthusiasm that only great cuisine and a full winter day's exertion can inspire. Tender strips of beef, pork, chicken, shrimp and a garden's worth of vegetables were dunked into the charcoal-heated firepot broth.

A step outside to the outhouse, a pause to watch the glowing canvas yurt against the black of the trees and the day was complete. I ducked back into the yurt and stretched out on my bed, the woodstove crackling an arm's length away.

Summertime on Minnesota's North Shore is no less enchanting. Come snowmelt, rivers that can be glimpsed in winter only through occasional holes in the ice tumble wildly over grand waterfalls and through mile after mile of steep rapids. Following heavy rains, rivers like the Baptism, Brule

89

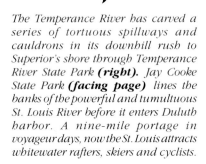

The Temperance River has carved a series of tortuous spillways and cauldrons in its downhill rush to Superior's shore through Temperance River State Park (right). Jay Cooke State Park (facing page) lines the banks of the powerful and tumultuous St. Louis River before it enters Duluth harbor. A nine-mile portage in voyageur days, now the St. Louis attracts whitewater rafters, skiers and cyclists.

the Mississippi watershed from the Great Lakes had to carry their large bark canoes and heavy loads of trade goods or furs seven miles to circumvent the cataracts. Ironically, some of the same rapids that were considered to be too treacherous for these hardy canoeists of the 17th and 18th centuries make great entertainment for today's weekend adventurers.

Rafters begin and end their experience on the St. Louis at the headquarters of Minnesota's only rafting company, Superior Outdoors, found along Minnesota Highway 210 about a mile east of Carlton. Mountain bike rentals and a kayak and canoeing instructional program are also offered by owner George Stefanyshyn (that rhymes with "definition") and his competent staff. Rafters are provided with life jackets and paddles and a shuttle service takes each group to the starting point near the town of Scanlon.

An orientation talk by the guides, who accompany the rafts in kayaks, is followed by a chance to practice maneuvering on a stretch of quiet water that precedes the first real rapid. This is a relatively benign chute of fast water emptying into a row of dancing "haystacks," one of which holds a regular shape upon which the guides love to surf in their kayaks much like surfers on their boards at the beach. After this initial test, the rapids on this section of the St. Louis grow progressively more difficult, testing paddlers' abilities to maintain control of their vessel amidst tossing waves and occasional submerged boulders.

The highlight of the run, without question, is a six-foot, river-wide plunge over a bedrock dike known as Electric Ledge. Even during relatively rare times of low water, the sheer drop of Electric Ledge, which is named after an overhead power line as well as the adrenaline-pumping sensations that the rapid evokes, provides for an exhilarating ride. A tongue of water at mid-stream allows the only clear passage through a melee of cascading water. Although guides stationed at the lip of the drop assure rafters that they are in the correct position, most fail to make the run without a good dousing of water, if not a momentary swim.

Below this rapid, the river splits around an island—over a 10-foot sheer waterfall on one side and down a rapid, "Little Kahuna," on the other. The latter route is the choice for rafters, who must negotiate another boulder garden that ends in a large surging wave. This excitement is followed by a final, smaller rapid and then a stretch of quiet water as the river flows into the Thompson reservoir. The sudden stillness, while paddling by pine-studded islands toward the waiting shuttle, is a welcome balm at the close of a wild ride.

and the Temperance fill their tight canyons with thunder and mist. These and many other smaller streams have hiking trails along their banks that lead to panoramic ridge-top overlooks. But if you really want to get intimate with all that water rushing madly toward Minnesota's inland sea, you'd do well to spend a sunny afternoon rafting one of the North Shore's largest rivers—the St. Louis.

The three-mile stretch of the St. Louis just upstream of the extremely violent rapids of Jay Cooke State Park, located in Carlton County about 20 miles south of Duluth, all were once part of the voyageurs' legendary "Grand Portage of the St. Louis." Fur traders who used this route to gain access to

Right: *It was because of the dangers posed by Superior's treacherous north shore that movers and shakers in the shipping industry persuaded Congress to build the Split Rock lighthouse in 1909. Having served its original function for 50 years—in the process becoming the most-visited light station in the country—Split Rock was deeded to the state in 1969 and now is a popular historic state park.*
Below: *The Witch Tree, Ma-ni-do Gee-shi-gance ("Spirit Little Cedar Tree") has been a revered North Shore landmark for centuries. This stunted and gnarled 400-year-old tree stands as a solitary sentinel on Hat Point, near the natural harbor of Grand Portage.*

Facing page: *Great Lakes shipping is the economic force that put the city of Duluth on the map, and at this largest inland sea port in the world, shipping primarily means iron ore. On a given day, spring through fall, there may be at anchor in the harbor several huge freighters from South America, Asia or Europe.*

Perhaps a less raucous exposure to the special charms of Minnesota's North Shore would be more to your liking. In addition to all the recreational opportunities to be found, the region is also rich in historical sites.

Duluth's harbor at the estuary of the St. Louis and its status of being at the head of the Great Lakes provides the city with the air of an international seaport—which it is, although it's 2,342 miles from the ocean. From ice-out in the spring until freeze-up each autumn, huge freighters from all over the world can be seen moored in the waters off Minnesota Point awaiting their turns at the docks. And there are two attractions along Duluth's waterfront that provide visitors with special insights into the shipping industry that has shaped the city's destiny.

The Canal Park Marine Museum located at the western end of Duluth's famed aerial bridge will give you an overview of the history of navigational efforts on the Great Lakes. Operated by the U.S. Army Corps of Engineers, the museum has exhibits and films chronicling the evolution of vessels that have plied Superior's waters, from the bark canoes of the Native Americans and voyageurs up to the most recent supertankers. There is a viewing area that overlooks the harbor and staff are on hand who can answer questions about any ships in sight. The geological history of

MICHAEL SILUK

Duluth's harbor at the estuary of the St. Louis River makes it an international seaport—even though it's 2,342 miles from the ocean.

the lake and aspects of the underwater marine environment also are introduced via film and displays.

Thus armed with some background to the subject, visitors can tour one of the *grand dames* of the shipping industry in a slip just south of the museum. Here the 610-foot S.S. *William A. Irvin,* from 1938 to 1978 the flag ship for U.S. Steel's fleet, the largest iron ore fleet in the world, has been set aside as a hands-on learning experience for the public. Visitors can get the real flavor of life aboard one of these gargantuan vessels: from the wood-paneled staterooms, lounge and dining room used by important stockholders, clients and other V.I.P. passengers in the bow—to the stern's sweltering engine room where, despite Duluth's moderate climate, summertime temperatures ranged from 100 to 115 degrees while underway.

Another historic site that was pivotal to the success of the shipping industry is Split Rock Lighthouse, now designated as a state park, found along the beautiful North Shore Scenic Drive 20 miles northeast of Two Harbors. Built in 1909 atop

an imposing 100-foot cliff soon after a particularly devastating storm brought down or damaged some 30 ships, the fog horn and beacon at Split Rock helped freighters keep their bearings on the lake. Split Rock served this role until the advent of advanced navigational technology in the late 1960s rendered the station obsolete.

However, as guides will tell you as you tour the immaculately kept facility and light-keepers' residences (there were three who, with their families, occupied this remote outpost in the early years), the construction of the light was actually a shrewd ploy concocted by steel magnates. These men—including the likes of Andrew Carnegie, John D. Rockefeller and J. Pierpont Morgan—persuaded Congress to spend tax dollars to build the light at Split Rock rather than implement the costly safe navigational procedures themselves. In addition to the very interesting tour of the light, a new interpretive center nearby has an excellent film on the history of the Split Rock Light and exhibits on life along the North Shore through the decades.

DANIEL J. COX

Right: Low evening sun casts wintry shadows over Norway pine and paper birch forest.

Facing page, left: For almost 20 years at the end of the 18th century, the fort at Grand Portage, now Grand Portage National Monument, was a rendezvous point for Canada's North West Company fur trading empire. Today, costumed guides tell tales of the lifestyles of these hearty voyageurs and their Scottish employers.

Right: It's easy to see why turn-of-the-century loggers chose to build an elaborate flume around High Falls on the Pigeon River rather than have their logs dashed to splinters by tumbling over the 120-foot drop—Minnesota's highest. Still, this Ontario-Minnesota border river's many violent rapids were so rough that a special low grade of lumber was developed to market boards made from Pigeon River logs.

Among the many ships that have met their ends beneath Superior's stormy seas—25 to 30 are known to have been lost along the North Shore alone—one, the *Madiera,* lies in relatively shallow waters within walking distance of the light house at Split Rock. This 500-foot, three-masted iron-ore tow barge, which lost one crew member when it succumbed to one of the worst blows of the century on November 28, 1905, lies badly broken up at the base of a cliff. On busy weekends at the park numerous sport divers can be watched as they prepare to descend to depths of 100 feet and more in order to explore the *Madiera's* shattered remains.

As if you were traveling back in time as you progress up the shore, just before crossing the border into Canada you reach the grandparent of historic sites in the Arrowhead region—one of Minnesota's oldest and most significant settlements, the National Park Service-operated Grand Portage National Monument. Grand Portage is interesting not just because of the physical site itself, but because of the incredible fur trading empire that it served from 1784 to 1803.

The tastefully reconstructed log buildings at Grand Portage and the surrounding rough-hewn log palisade are in a truly spectacular setting. Driving north on Route 61 through the Grand Portage Indian Reservation, you suddenly crest a hill to see the historic site sheltered on three sides by mountains and occupying a prime position along the shore of a large bay. On a clear day you can see the misty silhouette of Michigan's Isle Royale National Park against the horizon.

Each summer during the height of the fur trade the open lake in front of Grand Portage saw the gradual approach of dozens of huge Montreal canoes bearing tons of trade goods from the warehouses of the North West Company headquarters in Montreal. The voyageurs and Scottish company partners in these canoes (each of which was capable of holding more than a dozen passengers when fully loaded) were ar-

riving at the end of a treacherous journey through Lakes Huron, Michigan and across the length of Superior—the largest freshwater lake in the world.

At the fort they were met by hundreds of other voyageurs and "wintering partners" who had spent the winter in remote outposts in the Canadian and American wilderness trading with bands of Native Americans. These traders from the western wilderness reached Grand Portage at the end of a nine-mile trail that circumvented the impassable rapids and waterfalls of the Pigeon River. When the two groups met for their annual rendezvous it was a time of great joy and wild celebration.

The empire established by the North West Company in this enterprise was truly awesome. It stretched from Montreal in the east all the way to the Pacific Ocean in the Canadian West and to the Arctic Ocean far to the north. Hundreds of hardy French-Canadian voyageurs labored under excruciating conditions—often carrying loads of more than 180 pounds over difficult portages and paddling 16 hours each day—to fulfill their contracts. And in the end these laborers earned about enough money in a year's time to be able to purchase one or two of the fur hats produced by the beaver pelts they struggled to help transport half way around the world. By the time the era of the fur trade came to an end as the once-insatiable European appetite for furs abated in the mid-1800s, the beaver populations of much of North America had been driven almost to extinction.

LAKE SUPERIOR'S MANY MOODS

DANIEL J. COX PHOTOS ABOVE AND BELOW

TOM TILL

DANIEL J. COX

CONNIE WANNER

A drive along Lake Superior's shoreline passes through old fishing villages, crosses turbulent rivers and skirts towering cliffs. Each bend in the road suggests new diversions—agate or icicle hunting, berry picking, following a footpath or ski trail that disappears into the forest. The ever-changing light and weather reveal further nuances of Superior's complex nature.

**St. Croix River
Stillwater
Taylors Falls
Hinckley
North West Company
Fur Post
Banning State Park**

*The St. Croix valley—birthplace of government and commerce in Minnesota—attracts visitors now just as it drew settlers and loggers 150 years ago. Many today come to enjoy one of five state parks along the river's banks, where hardwood and pine forests mingle (**above**). Downstream of Taylors Falls (**facing page**), cruise and power boats join canoes to explore the river's clear waters.*

THE ST. CROIX VALLEY

In the suburban St. Paul neighborhood where I grew up, a rite of spring was conducted each year for the benefit of the male members of each family. It was called the Fathers and Sons Canoe Trip.

Starting when I was eight, as Memorial Day weekend approached Dad would unearth his World War II-vintage duffle bags and I'd help stuff them with a couple of changes of clothes, rain ponchos, flashlights, a stash of licorice and comic books, mosquito repellant, two cotton sleeping bags with hunting scenes adorning their felt liners and a canvas tent big enough to suit a Bedouin prince. Then we packed everything into the Titcombs' station wagon (or was it the Weeds'?) and set out on a journey that was ripe with the most delicious expectations. We were going to that almost mythical pine-scented place—a destination rather than a mere direction: North.

There would be bears. Fish. Campfires and wood smoke. And running through it all, the cold, fast-flowing waters of the St. Croix River. For three days that year and for several years to come the St. Croix would lure us ever farther downstream, over rapids and around bend after promising bend.

I sensed even then that the ancient commerce between a white-water river and a canoe is an enchanted one. The St. Croix was as moody, complex and elusive as a person. In the course of its journey it wound between thickly wooded banks through boulder gardens, danced with evident cheer across shallow gravel bars and suddenly plunged from the lip of a dam to enter a steep-walled canyon with swirling rapids. Then, just as unexpectedly, all that fluid chaos stilled itself to flow in reflective silence for its final, more gentle run to mingle with the much siltier Mississippi River at Hastings.

Needless to say, I was far from being the first person to find the natural features of the valley of the "holy cross" so alluring. In fact, it was in this valley that a group of foresighted pioneers gathered in 1848 to establish Minnesota's territorial status. The site they chose for this historic event was Stillwater—a lovely river town rich in 19th-century historic and architectural traditions that still prides itself as being the "Birthplace of Minnesota."

At the time of the territorial convention, the upper St. Croix watershed—which supported a vast expanse of towering white pine—had already begun to experience the effects of the sawyer's blade. When the first lumber mill was established in the little hamlet of Marine in 1838 it was estimated that the big pine were inexhaustible. By 1850 this optimism gave way to reality: by then it already was evident that the region's pine forests would be completely consumed by the end of the century.

In 1877, a writer with the *Mississippi Valley Lumberman* warned the lumber barons that in their "haste to grow rich," they were "ruthlessly sacrificing nature's pristine beauty to inordinate selfish greed." (Quoted in James Taylor Dunn's *State Parks of the St. Croix Valley.*) Such warnings went unheeded, however, and between the years 1839 and 1898 loggers cut 10.3 billion log feet of timber from the area. All these logs were floated downriver to the mills at Stillwater. In the process, huge log jams occasionally formed on the St. Croix—especially at a sharp bend in the river near Taylors Falls in the middle of the beautiful St. Croix Dalles.

Some 10,000 years ago, this deep canyon was cut through a dense basalt bedrock formation by the action of a voluminous river that drained Glacial Lake Duluth—a much larger predecessor to today's Lake Superior. As the river currents spun large boulders in their eddies, gaping pot holes and kettles were carved into the rock.

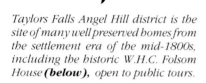

Taylors Falls Angel Hill district is the site of many well preserved homes from the settlement era of the mid-1800s, including the historic W.H.C. Folsom House (below), open to public tours.

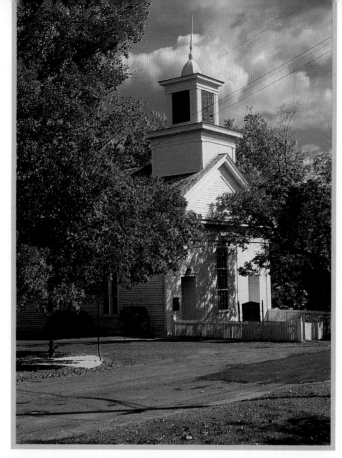

ABOVE: CHRIS POLYDOROFF; BELOW: TIM GRAY

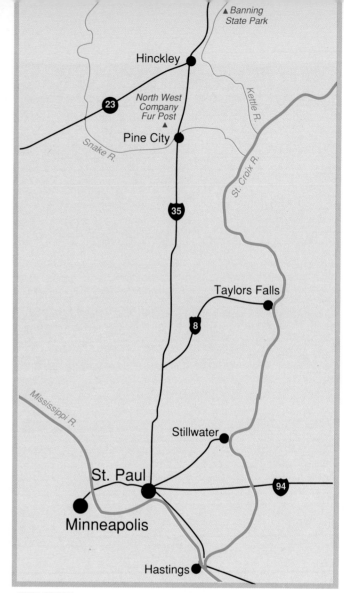

LINDA COLLINS

Today, many of these unusual geological formations can be seen in Interstate State Park in Taylors Falls. Often their walls are occupied by rock climbers challenging themselves by clambering up surface cracks and fissures. In the middle of the Dalles a short stretch of rapids has been preserved, which in summer and early fall is a favorite play spot for kayakers and whitewater canoeists.

The town of Taylors Falls offers a glimpse into the lifestyle of one of the area's early loggers who saw some

Left top: *Potholes carved by swirling water into the basalt bedrock in Interstate State Park near Taylors Falls hark back to post-glacial times when torrents fed by glacial Lake Duluth (occupying the same basin as Lake Superior today) rushed through a narrows now called the Dalles.*

Above and left: *The Hinckley Fire Museum, which occupies the town's old railroad depot, is a memorial to the incredible logging boom that started in the mid-1800s and which took such a heavy toll on the St. Croix valley and environs. Once blanketed with giant red and white pine, the area was clear-cut and covered with slash piles of brush and branches. In 1894, some 320,000 acres of tinder-dry land burned in a fire storm that destroyed the town of Hinckley, killing 418 people.*

financial success for his labors. The W.H.C. Folsom House, a Greek Revival home built in 1855, has a commanding view of the town and the river valley from the perimeter of the historic Angels Hill residential district. Tours of the Folsom House with its period furnishings give a sense of upper-middle-class family life in the second half of the 19th century.

Just down the street at 102 Government Road, on the other hand, you can get a feeling of how the other half lived. Built to handle occasionally unruly and besotted loggers

101

Historic sites abound in the St. Croix Valley, pointing to the beginnings of commerce in Minnesota.

CHRIS POLYDOROFF PHOTOS BOTH PAGES

who inundated the town during the annual lumber drives, the historic Taylors Falls jail has been tastefully converted into one of Minnesota's most unusual historic bed-and-breakfast establishments. From the fact that the jail was built of sandwiched two-by-fours, one might conclude that there was no great need for security—which may say something about the sorry condition of its tenants. At any rate, today's inmates should find it a most comfortable place to do time.

As the lumberjacks finished their work in the St. Croix region, they left in their wake a desolated landscape that was ripe for a further scourge: forest fire. Where virgin pine forests once stood, there remained huge slash piles of discarded limbs and underbrush, just waiting for the right conditions for a massive conflagration.

The summer of 1894 was particularly hot and dry, and residents of Pine County had had to cope with a number of small fires, many of which were ignited by sparks from

passing steam locomotives. Then on September 1 one of these fires was fanned by a hot, dry wind and a fire storm swept across the county. When it was over, 320,000 acres of land had been torched, 413 people killed and five towns burned to the ground.

Hinckley, one of those incinerated communities, has dedicated its old railroad station to the commemoration of this horrific event. The Hinckley Fire Museum, at 106 Old Highway 61, has photos, a multimedia presentation, a large mural and a collection of various household artifacts—many partially melted—to give some sense of what the experience was like.

Two more nearby historic sites recount other early industries that played important roles in the area's past. Two miles west of Pine City on Pine County Road 7, visitors can return to the first decade of the 19th century when the Snake River, a tributary of the St. Croix, supported an active fur trade. A partner with the Canadian North West Company and a small group of voyageurs spent two trading seasons inside the original log palisade (a reconstruction stands today) that surrounds The North West Company Fur Post. Sleeping at night in their tiny beds, cooking over the open fire, trading by day with local bands of Ojibway Indians, these men passed the winter here. In the spring they paddled up the St. Croix and down the Wisconsin Brule River to rendezvous with their fellows at Fort William on the north shore of Lake Superior.

The other historic site is found deep in a spectacular canyon of the Kettle River in Banning State Park. The Kettle, another valley carved by a powerful river draining Glacial Lake Duluth, is distinguished by its exposed sections of sandstone bedrock. Over thousands of years the glacial meltwater eroded in this bedrock, creating formations similar to those found at Interstate State Park—the distinctive kettles thus formed have given the river its name.

About the time of the Hinckley fire, entrepreneurs from the Twin Cities took notice of the Kettle River sandstone and set up a quarrying operation that commenced just before the turn of the century. The stone's strength and warm colors were considered excellent and the enterprise was a quick success. Sandstone secured at Banning, as the quarry site and village of 300 became known, can be seen today at the Minneapolis City Hall and at the historic James J. Hill House in St. Paul. Then, just as suddenly as it started, in 1905 the operation came to a halt. The emergence of structural steel as the preferred technology for building captured the market for sandstone, and Banning quickly became a ghost town.

Today a hike alongside the tumultuous rapids that flow through the Kettle's Hells Gate gorge leads to the Banning ruins. The remains of a power plant, sluiceways and the foundations of several other buildings stand near the river. against the steep cliffs, blocks of sandstone, piled like giant children's blocks, remain as evidence of the once-active quarry.

For walking or driving tours of Stillwater's outstanding architecture, call the Stillwater Chamber of Commerce at 612-439-7700.

Left and below: Banning State Park was formed along a particularly tumultuous stretch of the Kettle River, which derives its name from the huge natural cauldrons eroded into the sandstone riverbank during post-glacial times. Ruins of an abandoned sandstone quarry town site also make for interesting exploration in the park.

Facing page: Voyageurs at the North West Company fur post, a living-history site near Pine City, teach visitors how to throw a tomahawk and start a fire using flint and steel, while spinning tales about how "they" spent their time at the post, occupied during the winter of 1804-1805.

BIBLIOGRAPHY

Books

Bury My Heart at Wounded Knee, Dee Brown, Bantam Books, 1970.

A Guide to the Architecture of Minnesota, David Gebhard and Tom Martinson, University of Minnesota Press, 1977.

Joseph N. Nicollet on the Plains and Prairies, translated and edited by Edmund C. Bray and Martha Coleman Bray, Minnesota Historical Society, St. Paul, 1976.

Minnesota: A Bicentennial History, William E. Lass, Norton, 1977.

Minnesota: Off the Beaten Path: A Guide to Unique Places, John G. Shepard, Globe Pequot Press, 1989.

Minnesota Travel Companion: A Unique Guide to the History Along Minnesota's Highways, Richard Olsenius, Bluestem Productions, 1982.

Minnesota Underfoot: A Field Guide to the State's Outstanding Geologic Features, Constance Jefferson Sansome, Voyageur Press, 1983.

Room at the Inn Minnesota: Guide to Minnesota's Historic B&Bs, Hotels and Country Inns, Laura Zahn, Down to Earth Publications, 1988.

State Parks of the St. Croix Valley, James Taylor Dunn, Minnesota Parks Foundation, 1981.

Agencies and Organizations

Department of Natural Resources Information Center, 500 Lafayette Road, St. Paul, MN 55155-4040; toll-free from within Minnesota, 800-652-9747 (ask for DNR); from the Twin Cities, 296-4776.

Minnesota Office of Tourism, 375 Jackson Street, 250 Skyway Level, St. Paul MN 55101-1810; toll-free telephone numbers: from outside Minnesota, 800-328-1461; from inside Minnesota, 800-652-9747; in the Twin Cities, 296-5029.

Not only is the St. Croix a haven for anglers, its remarkably clear waters support one of the nation's healthiest and most diverse populations of freshwater mussels.

CHRIS POLYDOROFF